Fantasy and the Human Spirit

BOOKS BY JOHN CHARLES COOPER

Wine in Separate Cups (with Charles Sauer)
Celluloid and Symbols (with Carl Skrade)
The Christian and Politics
Paul for Today
Getting It Together
Religion After Forty
Finding a Simpler Life
The Roots of Radical Theology
Radical Christianity and Its Sources
The New Mentality
The Turn Right
Religion in the Age of Aquarius
A New Kind of Man
The Recovery of America

FANTASY

and the

HUMAN SPIRIT

John Charles Cooper

A Crossroad Book
THE SEABURY PRESS · NEW YORK

The Seabury Press
815 Second Avenue
New York, N.Y. 10017

Copyright © 1975 by John Charles Cooper
Printed in the United States of America

LIBRARY OF CONGRESS CATALOGING IN PUBLICATION DATA

Cooper, John Charles.
  Fantasy and the human spirit.
  "A Crossroad book."
  1. Conduct of life. 2. Fantasy. I. Title.
BJ1581.2.C63   170'.202   74-34567
ISBN 0-8164-0264-7

For Chauncey Miller Cooper,
My Father

Long before there was
Television to entertain,
He kept his children
Spellbound with his stories.
It takes little to be a good
Story teller, only the courage
To stand up to life and say,
    "I Am".
He has that courage.

Stranger

I'm not the person you think I am.
I'm not the person I used to be.
My inner story suddenly rose up,
Took possession and decided to be me.

Contents

Fantasy and the Human Spirit

Introduction

GOD, LIFE STORIES, AND FANTASY

Books are supposed to be informative, I know. But this is actually about you, your life story and your fantasies.

The Old Testament writer, Ecclesiastes (or the Preacher), who is often identified with Solomon, declared that men do have a life story, with a time for everything, good and bad. You are familiar with the words, for many of our young people have taken them up almost as a confession of faith in life. I like these words, too, but much more than believing that there is a general life story—a plan—for all men, I believe that each one of us has his own personal, inner life story—unique to ourselves, freely chosen for ourselves. Each one of us not only has a story to tell the world (our outer profession or vocation or mission) but we have an inner life story that we spend all our lives telling to ourselves alone.

The whole idea of an inner life story came to me through reflection upon my own inner life. I recalled the "stories" we told ourselves and acted out as children and began to notice that we might still as adults be doing the same thing. I was aware of the current notion of "parent tapes" and "scripts," but I have something deeper—and life-long—in mind. Our inner life story is the content of our most private level of consciousness. It is the actual reason, the final basis of the decisions we make—decisions that are often so baffling to others.

We not only *have* an inner life story, we *are* our inner life story, which forms the plot, the outline of our innermost, most private fantasy lives. I cannot prove this to you, except to say that I know myself to have such an inner story, but I am sure that I don't have to prove it anyway—you can prove it to yourself by a moment's reflection. And that may not even be necessary, for by an immediate intuition, most people that I have broached this insight to have confessed that it is true.

But what has all this to do with religion? With God? I would suggest it has everything to do with them, for our religious posture in the world is determined, in the end, by the kind of life story we are telling ourselves, by the kind of story we actually are. Religious books or religious services mean very little to us or to God, I feel, if they do not touch the inner story we are telling—for the only other one in the cosmos who knows the theme of our inner story is God. Perhaps only God compares what we say publicly with what we say to ourselves in our hearts. Religion is vain that concentrates only on the outer life of man, on conduct and public confession and words, forgetting that true faith is the attitude of the inner man towards God and the recognition of the silent attitude of God towards the inner man. We lose the genuine religious spirit and wander off into fruitless outer works and silly verbal conventions when we forget that God looks upon the hearts of men and women.

Such an insight is the burden of the preaching of the great Hebrew prophets, of Jesus, Paul, Augustine, of Martin Luther, John Wesley, and George Fox. Paint the outer temple as pure as we will, if the inner man with his inner story does not include absolute dependence upon God, what John Calvin called submission to the Divine, then we are merely hollow drums, not singers in the resounding chorus of the universe.

An emphasis upon our being identical with our inner story, with our fantasy life, goes well with young people, too. For it is in youth that we fasten upon the central themes of our inner story as a wandering shellfish fastens itself upon a coral fan in a tropic sea. Youth go through a confusing period of life when they try on one inner story after another, searching for a tale that will fit them comfortably while still being challenging and interesting. But one must be careful of the stories one tries out and use insight in the final choice of personal story. We should all beware of choosing too safe, too drab, or too dull an inner fantasy. If we do, we will only bore ourselves and disappoint others. In time, we will be forced to throw over our stories and burst free, hurting ourselves and others in the process.

Make adventure, love, concern, thoughtfulness, and an aggressive interest in life parts of your story. But do not mistake the lure of the outlaw's story for adventure—be careful of incorporating destructive elements in your fantasies, for such symbols lead not to fulfillment and adventure but only to self-destruction. Yes, youthful choices have a great deal to do with our inner life stories, with our fantasies and with our relation to God. Where our treasures—our dreams—are, there will our hearts be also.

1

Life Scenarios

OUR OWN PERSONAL LIFE STORY

Standing by the ferry point on the River Han in September, 1950, I glanced at a Marine riding cockily upon the barrel of a 155 millimeter gun. His legs were wrapped around the huge artillery piece, his head was tilted back, and on closer inspection, I could see that his eyes were closed. The Marine Corps was not large in those days, so it was no great miracle that I recognized this man as a companion from boot camp days. I shouted at him, "Jersey, what are you up to?" He lazily opened his eyes, looked at me in recognition and said, "Telling myself a story."

Years later, I noticed my wife swinging in a hammock with a satisfied expression on her face. Like all curious people I had to pry. "What are you doing?" I asked. "Telling myself a story," she answered.

You undoubtedly have had the same experience many times. A child sits by a frosted window, his lips moving. Perhaps his eyes are closed, too, or else he looks dreamily into the snowy distance. "What's up, Paul?" you ask. "I'm telling myself a story," or "I'm playing make-believe" might well be the child's reply. This may be true of your life, too. You, too, if you have ever awakened to consider your own reveries, you have probably found yourself "telling a story" in the immemorial fashion of the human race.

Human history was born in just that way. Men telling themselves a story began to tell their stories to each other. The myths, sagas, legends and poems, the traditions of all peoples began when one's personal story was merged by the continual and concerted efforts of many people over long reaches of time into the story of the clan, the tribe, the culture.

Hannah Arendt has observed that the cities of Greece were formed by the veterans of the Trojan War so they would have a place to tell their stories.[1]

Hans Ruesh, writing in *Back to the Top of the World*, has convincingly shown that man cannot live alone. We need each other even more than we sometimes fear each other. It takes at least two to survive. Not least of all, it takes two to talk to each other—to keep each other sane in the long, cold nights of life. Ruesh tells us of Papik, the Eskimo, who was threatening to go off on the ice alone:

"Hah!" he snorted. "Who needs a woman? A man only wants dogs."

He was wrong and he knew it. Nobody knew better than he that in the arithmetic of arctic life the smallest unit was the couple. But he couldn't acknowledge it, with all those eyes riveted on him in fascination. He had never felt prouder of being a Man, never more defiant of everybody and the world, and ready for the impossible.

"Papik!" Vivi pleaded. "The only females you can find up there are among the bears—and they will eat you." [2]

We are fascinated by the stories of others. We want to know all we can about the world around us. We want to reach out and encompass the adventures and life histories of those we meet. The wandering story teller, the singing minstrels, the blind or drunken poets who cross and re-cross the wine-colored seas of history's pages hold a fascinating attraction for us. Our human curiosity makes the poet and writer, the dramatist and moviemaker, both possible and necessary. Mankind does not now, nor has it ever lived by bread, or meat, or energy sources alone. Mankind also lives by the word—the story it tells itself in twenty-four-hour installments, year after year, century by century.

When someone passed by our battlelines in the war, we always shouted, "What's the word?" Sitting in the peaceful dorm of a college, the question is the same whenever a person pushes open the door. Waiting to hear who was elected to what, or how the moon launch went, or what Henry Kissinger did today, we naturally ask, "What's the word?" "What's the story?" In the beginning was the word—with God—and with man, the desire to know the word.

FROM THE OUTER TO THE INNER

In modern times, most studies of man, including studies in religion and theology, have started outside the individual person, concentrating on exterior, social forces. The inner life of the person—beyond what is necessary as an hypothesis to explain one's behavior—has been forgotten. We have forgotten that one's posture in the world (including a person's religious outlook) is the outgrowth of the inner story that one spends one's whole life telling oneself. The sociological, materialistic approach has been considered not only good social science but good psychology and good literary criticism as well. We have abandoned the ancient, magical way of approaching man, which starts with the inner nature and status of the individual rather than with the environment. We have not looked first at whether our own hearts are pure (or asked if the other person's is) but have sought to reckon the number of dollars or the size of the regiments we have to work with before taking on a challenge.

The monk, seeking salvation in the caves of the desert, knew something else. The medieval alchemist, who sought to purify himself within, knew better. The fledgling knight, who spent a long night in prayer upon his armor, knew differently. That the issues of life flow out of the inward spirit, earlier ages knew. In our time we are learning that again.

Of late, psychologists and theologians, writers and moviemakers have returned to this older way of understanding man. We feel, even when we cannot know, that men are interested in other people's stories, and want to know the latest word—so that they can relate that information to the primary touchstone of their life—their own inner story, their personal fantasy world, the place where human beings live.

Each of us has a much more basic thing going for us than either social role expectation or "parent tapes" or prejudices. We have, at the bottom of our minds, our own freely chosen personal fiction, our own fantasy life—the story that we tell to ourselves alone and try to make come true. As children this story kept us warm; we clung to it when the multicolored visions of nightmares filled our silent rooms.

Our problem is that we are so often ignorant of our own natures. We have repressed, forgotten, screened out the very juices of our life for so long, that it is difficult to recognize our own inner image as it is reflected off the dull, materialistic veneer of our minds. We have to re-learn the old truths of the heart, the old understandings of the self, again. We must remember that Jesus firmly taught that "unless you become as little children, you shall not enter the Kingdom."

Miguel de Unamuno, like most existentialists, wanted to wake men from sleep. Like Jean Paul Sartre, who seemed determined to pop our every precious and protecting bubble, Unamuno felt that men and women ought to be awake, to face the gray and cheerless day, to do their duty.

The age of Stoic, muscular existentialism is gone. Today we once again want to sleep, to dream the dreams of the sorcerer's apprentice, to see the visions of a sleepy, lustful Faust. Even our waking hours are full of the names and symbols of the Devil himself, of Baal, Beelzebub, and Lucifer, or, on the other hand, of the Holy Ghost, the risen Jesus, and the angels of the Apocalypse.

The seven seals of the Revelation are broken, not guarded; we plunge into the eschatological depths; we no longer sail upon the crystal waters of calm reason. Images, dreams, and myths, symbols in every stage of dress and undress, present themselves. A theologian, David Miller, seriously writes that the church itself should reconsider and publicly embrace polytheism. Zeus and Hercules, Apollo and Dionysius mingle with the eroding soil and the contaminated sea. A supernatural revolution washes over psychology. Vulcan and the polluted air merge in front of our dreaming eyes, but our dreaming innocence is gone. The eruption of our fantasy life upon the stage of history has given us a recognition of who we are and whither we are tending. Fantasy now is no longer play, but therapy.

MIND, NOT MATTER, THE MARK OF WHAT WE ARE

Our typical turn of mind is to homogenize all men into one pattern and to see the vast differences between them merely as matters of technological development. The way we think determines the way we live, rather than vice-versa. People in Oceania and Africa differ from people in New York City (if at all) in terms of worldviews, the way they think, not just in the surroundings in which they make their living. It is the head, not the hands that make one people different from another.

Not only Polynesians, but New Yorkers and Midwesterners, too, dream of the rituals of initiation, fertility, sacrifice, purification, and salvation. So-called "modern" Western man also is a trafficker in the symbols and myths that have characterized man from earliest times. We have our dreams of transcendence and our nightmares of fear as well as the "primitive" peoples of the Amazon Basin. The commercial success of the movies, *Rosemary's Baby* and *The Exorcist*, demonstrates this quite well. Movies and books like these are able to take the ancient symbols literally and set them down in the context of apartment houses in Manhattan and bungalows in Georgetown and still be believable for tens of millions of twentieth-century people. Scratch the surface of our urban sophistication and the forest dwellers' sensibilities appear. Authors and directors are capable of doing this because they deal in symbols and myths that by-pass the conscious rationalism by which we think and guide our daily lives. The cult of the Great Mother, symbolized in Mary, is alive and well under the heavy theology of the reforming Catholic Church; Baalism, with its love of the homeland, lingers under the de-mythologization of the modern Protestant Church. We live not only in the late twentieth century after the Christ-event; we also live—at one and the same point, at one and the same "time," in the eternal nowness of mythology. The Fall is now, the Flood is now, the Covenant is now, and the Lamb slain from the foundation of the world, dying and rising again, is being overcome and overcoming now.

The sermons of the late Martin Luther King, Jr. realistically utilized the symbols of Egyptian bondage and God's grace-given Exodus, becoming more powerful, not less, because of this ancient touchstone. The mystery of Bread and Wine, Body and Blood, remains no less attractive and mysterious in English and French than it was in Latin. The inkwell that Luther threw at the devil in 1520 has not yet hit the solid wall in our day of exorcism-fever. Athanasius still chides Arius, though both are shifting dust in the warm sunlight of the Mediterranean area, every time the creed is chanted in public worship. The time of truth is always, and eternally, now.

Richard L. Rubenstein[3] and Harvey Cox,[4] coming, respectively, from the Reformed Jewish and Free Church Protestant Christian perspectives, agree that religion today ought to re-examine its "modern" outlook on ritual and ceremony. Even the highly educated want and need ritual. In the face of Dachau, Bergen-Belsen, Hiroshima, and My Lai, all that the sensitive person can do is raise the prayers for the dead. We need ritual, we need prayer, and we need to express the ancient symbols publicly and together. Modern people confess that they often feel possessed by demons. Even men who walked on the moon feel the urge to live in the dimension of the Spirit. Without paying attention to the symbols within us, which, cast in mythological form, are the real ground of meaning for us, we can neither understand that personal story which we are nor make sense of the story our human group is writing—in the pages of the newspaper—as mankind creates history.

I believe we can catch more than a glimpse of the ancient myths and symbols if we reflect upon that silent conversation we are constantly carrying on with ourselves. I think that we are talking to ourselves all the time, awake and asleep, telling ourselves a story. This story moves forward even when our outer attention is directed elsewhere. We turn from it to do our work, to watch television, to read a book, forget our story for a while, then find it still going on when we return. When we fall asleep, the story goes on in dreams that only mark the top of a dark pyramid of unconscious activity deep within the brain.

LIFE SCENARIOS

In this open-all-day, all-night, continuous-playing, inner cinema, different roles flash by, played by the same person at different periods in his life, and by different people. A few people even seem to be trying to tell more than one story to themselves at one and the same time. In all these cases the various roles are actually life scenarios, plans for the story we are telling ourselves. While there are many, indeed an uncounted number, of life scenarios—from the mighty hunter scenario of primitive tribesmen to the astronaut scenario of modern children—I offer the following few as significant examples.

The first three scenarios—the Soldier of Fortune, the Explorer, and the Wounded Healer—are deeply embedded in Western consciousness. They are basic scenarios and share many aspects in common. Amazingly, they also share much with the tragic hero of ancient Greek mythology. The tragic hero is a hero precisely because of his above-average striving, and he is tragic just because he has an inner flaw that secretly destroys him when he reaches the pinnacle of worldly success. In a fashion, both the Wounded Healer and the Soldier of Fortune share in the tragic hero's major characteristics. As we shall see later, the Magician, too, shares some of these elements. This is true because all these scenarios concern lives of heroism marked by a fatal—or near-fatal—weakness. Perhaps of all tragic fantasies, the Soldier of Fortune is the most flawed, the most driven, the most unsatisfied. Dissatisfaction may well be the groundwork for the inner quest that drives man to create civilization and seek to find God. In turning to the first of these scenarios, we shall look at the perennial heroic story, the ruthless but ultimately unsuccessful inner story of the Soldier of Fortune.

The Soldier of Fortune

The Soldier of Fortune, spinning his life scenario from his inward psychic forces, starts out as an extrovert and ends as an introvert. The Soldier of Fortune begins with a search for outward adventure, thrills, pleasure, in the company of others and before others. Gradually, by moving from adventure to adventure, war to war, woman to woman, the Soldier ends up alone.

The Soldier of Fortune is an adventurer of the body, of feats of arms, of strength and comradeship. He is the pure extrovert—with apparently little spiritual depth. His fantasies embrace struggle and combat, tests of endurance and of resoluteness. The Soldier may seek to help others, but out of a desire to act out his resoluteness and courage in front of others. This particular life scenario is, I think, very prevalent among young males in Western society. It is acted out every day in Boy Scout troops, National Guard units, the active armed forces, and even by some political leaders. Millions of younger and older men, engrossed in camping, hiking, skiing, mountain climbing, hunting, fishing, boating, and flying, are acting out the Soldier of Fortune scenario. Indeed, the whole drama of courtship and romance and of promiscuous sexuality is firmly based upon it.

Hot rod racers, motorcycle gang members, pro football players all generally fit the Soldier of Fortune scenario. The clearest weaving of this psychic fabric into external dress, into acting out, is the lifestyle of the Hell's Angels. The quest for dragons, combat, and sex is directly portrayed in the motorcycle gang's cruising up and down the roads looking for "action." The affectation of leather and chains brings to mind the armored knights of old. The use of the swastika, Nazi army helmets and iron crosses shows the aggressive military mystique behind the whole lifestyle. Yet the motorcyclist is interested in motors, beer, fun, and girls, along with a majority of other males. He differs in degree, not in kind from other young men.

A portion of the Soldier scenario is part of almost every male. But in the person who is chiefly determined by the

Soldier of Fortune fantasy, the romantic quest never ends. In time, the search for sensual enjoyment is transmuted into a quest for honors and glories—but the inner dynamics of the myth remain the same. The Soldier fantasy has not really changed since Jason and the Golden Fleece or Odysseus and the Trojan War.

If history is a record of more wars than acts of healing, more towers lifted above the clouds of mankind's Babels than the building of arks, it is because the Soldier of Fortune is such a deep-seated aspect of our myths, symbols, and inner lives. The sword has often been identified even with the cross, and due to its sharpness has often supplanted it. What is the Crusader Knight but the Soldier of Fortune sprinkled with holy water? What is the quest for the Holy Grail by Arthurian Knights but the substitution of the way of the sword for the way of the cross? From the preaching of the children's crusade to the proclamation of Christian anti-Communism the inner dynamics are the same: the Soldier of Fortune, restless, aggressive, acquisitive, and curious, baptized with a virtue he does not deserve.

I have always been fascinated by the Soldier of Fortune's story, no doubt because it is so much a part of my own inner story, but knowing him so closely I cannot but distrust him when he is cloaked in predestinated righteousness. The Soldier of Fortune, well understood, is precisely not righteous, rather he is the loner, the odd man out, the drifter, the outlaw, the pioneer. Looked at with open eyes that take in the inner turmoil, the basic unhappiness that drives him, the Soldier of Fortune is no saint, but if you are a rough and ready kind of person yourself, he can be a good companion. Looked at clearly, with his muddy boots, unshaved face, and fatigue-rimmed eyes, he is a human being that a life of hard knocks has led me to appreciate. But the Soldier of Fortune is no savior. Like his archetype in the gospels, the centurion at Capernaum (Matt. 8:5–13), he needs a savior badly. Like his colleagues, the publicans and other sinners, he often recognizes the voice of a healer and sometimes he responds. When I was a boy, I heard the old sailors talk of settling down and buying a chicken farm. The Roman government, long ago, gave the retired legionnaire his little farm on the frontier. It may be that the vision of that little farm lies deep within the foolishness and the nobility of humanity's risk-takers, the Soldiers of Fortune, even today.

The Explorer

The Explorer myth, the fantasy of the adventurer in the service of science, is an academically conditioned version of the Soldier of Fortune fantasy. The Explorer can go everywhere he wishes with a clean conscience, for he serves the higher good of man not just his own sensual (and intellectual) interest. The Explorer, in the best-of-all-worlds fashion of a rationalistic philosopher, combines the impact of the Teacher with the thrills of the Soldier of Fortune.

Who has not wanted to be an Explorer? This fantasy is a refuge of the thrill-deprived in every town, in every generation. Such human needs have created the great demands for the products of the writer's research and imagination, and form the bedrock of Hollywood's cinema, Broadway's stage, and television's adventure movies. The Explorer's bible, *National Geographic*, lies everywhere, in public schools, hospitals, doctors' offices and homes.

The Wounded Healer

The basic contrast between the Soldier of Fortune or the Explorer and the Wounded Healer lies in the difference between the extroverted and introverted personality. The Wounded Healer starts out as an introvert and works outward to become an extrovert. Having sought healing for himself (as Jesus did in the baptism, the temptations, the transfiguration experience), the healer ("Savior") then seeks to heal others. He is a sublimated introvert.

The Wounded Healer is an adventurer of the spirit, a voyager of the mind and emotions. He is, in fact, the very basis of Christian faith. The Book of Hebrews presents Jesus as a Wounded Healer in clear terms. The effect of this presentation on the psychic history of man is incalculable.

The unknown author of this epistle speaks simply of "Jesus," again and again. Jesus is presented as man and as more than man. He moves through a process of growth, becoming superior to angels, inheriting titles greater than theirs (Heb. 1:4). Because of Jesus' character, God anoints him to be above all other men (Heb. 1:9). Jesus is adopted, we are tempted to say, "made to sit at God's right hand," "crowned with glory" (Heb. 2:9). So Jesus is named by God as a high priest (Heb. 5:10).

The continuity of Jesus with all other men is also stressed (Heb. 2:11; 1:14). But this man among men, so singled out by God, was also destined to be both priest and sacrifice. His personal fantasies must have been confusing, if he saw himself as both the sacrificing priest and the sacrificial lamb. Ralph Waldo Emerson has the Hindu god say, "I am the slayer and the slain" in his poem, "Brahma." The Jesus of the Book of Hebrews (and of passages in Paul) could have said the same.

Jesus comes across as a genuine Wounded Healer—one who is able to help because he has himself been hurt. The demons know Jesus (Mk. 1:34) and Jesus knows the demons. He has fought them again and again, from the desert to the cross. He has suffered, fasted, prayed, and emerged victorious in his confrontation with the powers of evil. The Tibetan shamans studied by Mircea Eliade are right: Only the man who has made the midnight journey to the moon, beyond the stars, and has fought the principalities and powers on their own terms and come back wounded can deal helpfully with spirits, with sickness, and with evil.[5]

Jesus was very good at describing other people's inner stories. The adulterous woman told others, "Come, see a man who told me all I ever did." Many preachers and scholars have tried to limn Jesus' secret story, too. Somehow, all the efforts to discover his secret or his idea of the Messiah or even his feelings about peace, war, sex, and wealth, fail to satisfy. Perhaps we should look at Jesus again and see what his story can tell us about ourselves.

What Was Jesus' Story?

Obviously I can no more read Jesus' mind and subconscious any more than the next person. But I can try to expose some of the Biblical material about Jesus that is often ignored, and try to let Jesus speak for himself. What was Jesus' inner story? Can we reconstruct the inner, personal story that Jesus spent his life telling himself? Was Jesus' story anything like the many stories about him that the church has told through the centuries?

The problem, simply stated, is, was there a Messianic secret in Jesus' life? Did he harbor an inner consciousness of being God's Messiah? And, whether he thought of himself as precisely "the Messiah" or not, what was the nature of Jesus' inner life? The later creeds declared he was "of a reasonable soul and body." But what was the secret of Jesus' soul?

Jesus' Inner Story

Everyone else tells Jesus' story for him. What would it be like to hear Jesus tell his own inner story?

Clearly, Jesus had one. Everyone has. But most people find their personal story ignored by others. Jesus, along with other controversial characters in history, did not have that problem. Everyone else was sure they knew what his inner story was, from his mother and family to Pontius Pilate. Even Peter presumed to tell Jesus how to live his life and wished to keep him from the cross (Matt. 16:21–23).

In turn, Jesus was put down as just another Galilean evangelist, the Son of Mary or Son of Joseph; as a teacher of heretical doctrine; as John the Baptist resurrected from the dead; as Elijah similarly raised, or some other revivified prophet; as a pretender to David's kingly throne; and as the Messiah sent by God. Which one of these scenarios, if any, did Jesus believe himself? This question has occupied Bible scholars for centuries.

In recent years, Jesus' story has been expounded to say he was a revolutionary (Zealot) or, at the least, an anti-establishment man. Jesus' traditional image as a prince among peace makers has also been stressed. He has been given strong heterosexual urges in the play, "Jesus Christ—Superstar" (which the ancients seem to have taken away), and in other literature has been accused of homosexuality.

Without going into the convoluted byways of New

Testament scholarship, let us simply say that Jesus' inner story shines through even the late and heavily edited texts of the gospels. Jesus saw himself as, and laid down as the plot and theme of his life, the scenario of a man totally dedicated to God. At the core of Jesus' innermost fantasies, he identified with the personal, caring, ethical-social God of the Old Testament and of Pharisaic tradition. "My meat and drink is to do the will of the Father" is the essence of Jesus' own story. It is as simple and as difficult as that.

I think the evidence—texts which lie like stones in a Judean field, scattered through many sections of the gospels—is conclusive. "Why do you call me good?" Jesus once asked. "No one is good but God alone." Jesus' inner story may have flown off into fantasies about the Son of Man and the end of the age, but it founded itself on this—his dedication to God. Jesus was more like Samuel than he was like David. He saw himself more as a prophet and priest than a king. Called from childhood, Jesus could rise to fury in defense of God's holiness, just as the aged Samuel hacked Agag to death when Saul refused to apply the ban to the captured Canaanites (I Sam. 15:33). A man of wisdom and peace, he was also capable of aggressive passion (Luke 22:36). Jesus was dedicated to God, not to a sect, a doctrine, or to either liberal or conservative ideas of what is right and wrong.

Jesus in the Gospel of Mark

While Jesus was the God-obedient man, like Samuel more a prophet/priest than a king, it seems that he was thought—by others—to harbor a secret concept of who and what he was. According to Mark's gospel, this secret kept coming out, for it was too big a secret (and too close to the truth) to hide.

We read in Mark 1:25, about a demon-possessed man Jesus healed, "But Jesus rebuked him, saying, 'Be silent, and come out of him.'" In Mark 1:34: "And he healed many who were sick with various diseases, and cast out many demons; and he would not permit the demons to speak, because they knew him." In Mark 1:44: ". . . and said to him, 'See that you say nothing to any one; but go, show yourself to the priest, and offer for your cleansing what Moses commanded, for a proof to the people.'" And in Mark 3:12: "And he strictly ordered them [the demons] not to make him known."

Again, in Mark 4:11: "And he said to them, 'To you has been given the secret of the kingdom of God, but for those outside everything is in parables.'" In Mark 5:43: "And he strictly charged them that no one should know this, and told them to give her something to eat." In Mark 7:36: "And he charged them to tell no one; but the more he charged them, the more zealously they proclaimed it." In Mark 8:30: "And he charged them to tell no one about him." In Mark 9:9: "And as they were coming down the mountain, he charged them to tell no one what they had seen, until the Son of man should have risen from the dead." (The climax of the "leaking" of the Messianic secret.)

Jesus' inner story was obviously one that grew out of a deep devotional life—one that was absolutely dedicated to the will of God. He saw himself as a proclaimer-teacher-healer who had to be wounded to achieve God's will.

"Christ Figures" as Wounded Healers

The Wounded Healer—the Suffering Servant of Isaiah 52–53—is essentially a Christ figure in that he is one who seeks to atone for sin. It is the self-sacrificial attitude of one who puts God's holiness above all else ("hallowed be thy name") and who puts the needs and lives (and souls) of others before his own ("greater love has no man than this, that he lay down his life for his friends").

There is a deep feeling in mankind that only one who has suffered the blows of life can aid other people when they undergo that test. The Book of Hebrews stresses this motif—that Christ has become a high priest for men by undergoing temptation. By suffering, men learn patience and compassion—or at least some do.

Also the ancient tradition of the Holy Man—the shaman, the guru, the spirit-doctor, the exorcist—is one in which the person endures trials that often leave him crippled in body and, perhaps, broken in mind—to be made holy is to be possessed by the divine spirit. Plato preserves the ancient Greek tradition that the prophet, the mouthpiece of the gods, is divinely mad. In the *Phaedrus*, Plato observes: "There are two kinds of madness; one produced by human infirmity, the other by a divine release from the ordinary ways of men." [6] And: "If the ancient inventors of names had thought madness a disgrace or dishonor, they would never have called prophecy, which is the noblest of the arts, by the very same name as madness, thus inseparably connecting them; but they must have thought that there was an inspired madness which was no disgrace." [7]

I wonder if it was this concept of madness that the Jews applied to Jesus in John 10:20? Or that his friends implied in Mark 3:21? If prophecy is a madness, then Jesus agreed with Plato and lived out that Samuel/prophet scenario, as did St. Paul later (Acts 26:24, 25).

Other Types of Healers

People observed that Jesus was "beside himself," that is, out of his body, or "mad," but also that power flowed from him, and he could cast out spirits. Jesus had wrestled in the desert with temptation. He had gone through the ordeal. Now, he could proclaim and heal. In the case of everyone who exercises the power of creativity, we must postulate a rich inner life. The achievement of making an impression on mankind can, humanly speaking, be laid at no other door than the teeming mind of the impressive, fully developed personality. Out of the day-dreaming of the scientist comes the new formula, the new machine, the new practical use for some bit of theoretical knowledge. Out of such dreams comes poetry, too, with its evocation of feelings in a tactile expression of language. Feelings, sensations, ecstasy, the touch of stone or wood, or flesh or steel, such is the power of the poet's words that we ourselves re-experience these same things in our own minds.

In the case of the prophet with his moral exhortation, or the priest with his ritual evocation of the sense of the sacred, the human spirit experiences a flash of recognition —a hint of how life hangs together, a conviction that the world's process has consistency and purpose. By extrapolation from such experiences we build up the geometry of thought and feeling—the creation of philosophies and religions. Jesus was such a poet of the spirit, a geometrician of human aspiration and dread—a prophet of man's sin and a priest of God's forgiving power.

Hundreds of reformed drunks, converted sinners who become evangelists, neurotic pastors who become counselors after their own treatment, and petty criminals who grow up to become moralists (remember St. Augustine?) confirm the Wounded Healer's saving function. Only those who have been close to the fire know how much it burns. And yet the pain in the soul is real and intense, and the tragic element in the life of the Wounded Healer is never overcome. "My God, my God, why have you forsaken me?" As the orthodox theologians of old said: "He who knew no sin became sin for us."

The Book of Hebrews is a delineation of the process by which Jesus moved forward to become the essential prophet-priest. Perhaps that is Jesus' inner story. Hebrews stresses the obedience of Jesus, his submission to the will of God. Ultimately, in the garden of Gethsemane he can put his inner story into words: "Nevertheless, not my will, but thy will be done." A submission ratified on the cross: "Father, into thy hands I commit my spirit." Jesus' inner story, and the theme of every fantasy that made it up was to be the first absolutely obedient man. That his life story integrated his obedience, thought, word, and deed, impressing itself upon the men of his time, and through them on all history, is beyond dispute. Therefore, we still look to Jesus as the author and perfector of our faith.

The Wounded Healer and the Modern Psyche

The Wounded Healer, the supremely religious personality, was considered deranged, psychically ill by Sigmund Freud. For Freud, religion was an illusion, and the binding of energy into religious beliefs and behavior patterns was commitment of the self to an hallucination. Most other psychiatric thinkers would not agree with Freud, indeed, thinkers like Jung say people wander mentally until they devote themselves to the questions addressed by religion.

The seeking of suffering for the sake of the experience of suffering, is rightly named an aberration, but the opposite tendency, to flee from every possible pain and difficulty, is equally aberrant. The Wounded Healer, the person made whole through suffering who now would aid others, is neither masochist nor coward. Such a person may be the only truly mature man or woman, since it is impossible to live long in this world without encountering pain, frustration, difficulty, and defeat.[8] Those who cannot cope with threat, pain, opposition, and failure drop out of the effective stream of personal and social life—dropouts we have all witnessed and which we have all experienced as temptations.

In the harsh winter of 1950, my regiment was surrounded by the CCF, the Chinese "volunteer" army that suddenly struck us at Hagaru in North Korea. The temperature was 30 degrees below zero Fahrenheit, and we had little food and ammunition. Constantly harassed by the enemy, always on the move southward along the rutted mountain roads, some men stood up under fire— unable to endure. The distressed husband who commits suicide when his affairs hit rocky ground and he is unsure of his family's support is a similar example. I can remember when the sight of a body wrapped in a sleeping bag and thrown on the back of a truck began to look less gruesome than inviting. The temptation of quitting is ever-present. I think I felt the lure of simply giving up most strongly, though, when I moved my family from the comforts of a little Southern college town to a cellar-like apartment on Chicago's South Side. Looking at my little children broken out with a rash of chicken pox they had picked up in their new setting, seeing the filth all over our things made turning back and quitting graduate school seem the right thing to do. I didn't lie down and die in North Korea or quit the University of Chicago. Most people don't. I don't think that makes us abnormal, but human.

The Wounded Healer, then, is not, in my evaluation, either mentally deranged or superhuman, but humanly mature. It is the essence of the Wounded Healer's scenario that he (or she) has harnessed the instinctual drives, lures, weaknesses, aversions, fears, and thoughtlessness. The Wounded Healer has developed his ego and his identity into a satisfying, efficient agent of dealing with the world—including other people. The Healer then elevates his working relation with the world into principles that become the essence of his superego. Jesus' life reveals much of this process. Not desiring to take advantage of others, Jesus elevates the rabbinic rule of social behavior into his chief ethical principle: Do unto others as you would have them do unto you. Not being filled with self-condemnation, Jesus refused to be caught up in condemning others. Judge not lest you be judged. Has no one condemned you? Neither do I condemn you. Go, and sin no more.

Everyone of us has a daily opportunity to become more attuned to the Wounded Healer's scenario. Frustration and disappointment are our lot in every portion of life. We can learn from our experience and learn compassion for other people caught in suffering, too, or we can flee from the reality of experience by hard-heartedness, indifference, or a psychotic break with the world. We should not seek suffering, but rather seek to learn from our experience of it when it comes, as it inevitably does.

The Prophet: News from Nowhere or God's Story of Us?

We have all seen the cartoonist's caricature of the prophet—a gaunt figure with long white robes and flowing hair, carrying a sign saying, "Repent." That such characters exist is a proposition no city dweller would dispute. Stand in Harvard Square and watch the young "Process" prophets handing out leaflets, or watch the Hare Krishna people dance and drum in the Chicago Loop (and sell their literature at O'Hare Field) and you can see that the fantasy of the prophet is very much alive. Turn on the television set and you can see why the eccentric elements of the prophet's role are so fascinating. It is hard to get excited by a middle-aged man wearing a Brooks Brothers suit, giving out platitudes to other well-dressed people. The financial success of books like Hal Lindsey's *The Late, Great Planet Earth*[9] shows the psychic need for the more unusual elements of prophecy. I would observe that the 1970's are a time of prophetic revolution; taking prophecy in a loose sense, to be sure.

The secularist is tempted to dismiss all prophecy as news from nowhere or at most the acted out inner fantasies of neurotics or psychotics. Yet millions of other people believe in one form of prophecy or another (Billy Graham, Hal Lindsey, Jeanne Dixon), seeing in prophetic announcements God's story of mankind, his message for us. There is a basis for this belief in the foundation documents of the Christian faith, the Old and New Testaments.

The overriding belief of the Old Testament is that God acts in the arena of history. God is not conceived as making the world and then leaving it to its own devices; rather God maintains a fatherly, directive role in the operation of the universe and in the affairs of men. The stories of Genesis concentrate on God's own work in choosing the people of Israel to be his light to the nations of the world. Exodus tells us of the covenant that the Lord established with Israel, and the writing prophets give an even wider picture of God's activity. Beginning with Amos, they saw God at work in other nations of the world as well as Israel, using all peoples to work out his will. The other prophets, Hosea, Isaiah, Jeremiah, etc., all continued in this world-embracing vein.

There are two confused concepts of prophecy, both in the Old Testament and at the present time. The first concept is that of the ecstatic, spirit-filled person who acts in unusual ways. Here Plato's conception of divine madness is to the point. Along with this idea goes the view of prophecy as prediction. People are anxious about the future and want to know how to prepare for it. The ecstatic prophet, from the priestess at Delphi to the false prophets at the court of Israel's kings to the many religious and occult prophets on the lecture circuit today, all played and play this role. Not surprisingly, such predictive prophets usually expound the old-time religion and call for conservative reaction or else the maintenance of the *status quo*. The person who feels that the world is morally decaying may very well develop the inner life story of such an ecstatic prophet. In a political sense, both Hitler and Mussolini were such prophets of the ancient, pagan virtues and opponents of new-fangled notions like Communism and modern art.

The other conception of the prophet is that of the person chosen by God to point out the moral failures of today in the name of the equally real moral opportunities. The writing prophets of the Old Testament were not reactionaries but represented a moral and social advance over their contemporaries. Amos and others did search the scriptures for a usable past, calling the people to the foundational beliefs of their religion in order for them to solve the problems before them. The life scenario of the true prophets was and is that of a check and balance on kings who acquire too much power and priests who reduce religion to ceremony and comfort.

Because the true prophet does attack the establishment, the way things are, he or she is often rejected and persecuted. This possibility does not frighten everyone, but makes the prophetic scenario all the more attractive. To feel one is doing a prophet's work (and therefore that one will receive a prophet's reward) is extremely ego-enhancing. For the strong personality it is a hard inner life story to beat, fortunately for the rest of the human race. Just as aristocrats sponsored the development of Renaissance art, the superiority complex has sponsored the rise in moral tone that is the mark of the higher religions and great civilizations.

The Wounded Healer and the Prophet have affinities with that aspect of culture we call religion, although both the Healer-fantasy and the prophet-fantasy are filled with intimations that one has a cosmic secret. There is another basic life scenario, similar to these of the Healer and the Prophet that is not necessarily connected to the religious dimension, but concentrates on knowledge. This is the life scenario of the Teacher.

The Teacher

Basically, the Teacher's life scenario grows out of the ancient shaman or witch-doctor role. As we recede back in time, we find that the Healer, the Teacher, and the Magician (more on him later) were all one person. By the passage of millennia of human experiences the various aspects of this role have been divided, appearing in several guises in our myths, dreams, day dreams, and inner fantasies. This is not entirely true of the inner life story of some, for the adoption of one life role (*e.g.*, the Wounded Healer or the Teacher sent from God) may include claims for all the functions of the ancient shaman, even though only one function (*e.g.*, the Teacher) is consciously adopted.

We should note that the modern, secular conception of the Teacher is an incomplete life scenario. At bottom, the one who feels the call to be a Teacher feels the call of a "Teacher sent from God." It is in this respect that Jesus became known as a teacher among his disciples. "By this we know that you are a teacher sent from God and need no one to tell you anything" (John 16:30). The public school teacher of today, in many instances, has lost this dimension of his inner life fantasy, while the college professor has tended to retain some of this depth dimension. The secular professor may view his call as from "the truth" rather than from God, but the inner dynamics are the same. This feeling of call often leads to the disputes between the sciences and the humanities, and between the various academic disciplines that mark university life.

Inner and Outer Attractions of the Teacher

Since I have spent my life as a teacher, I would like to explicate the life scenario of "The Teacher" more fully. There are two drawing powers in the ideal or symbol of the teacher—the inner (the attraction of self-development) and the outer (the attraction of the student). A number of other elements figure in the overall attractiveness of the teacher as a model for a life scenario. From the inner side there is the quest for discovery of the truth, the lure of remaining young in spirit by continual study and by association with other scholars and students. From the outer side there is the security of the teacher's status, and the coveted ability to help, to guide, even to heal others. Above all, there is the lure of the subject matter and the push of the great emptiness of the mind—the feeling that one does not really know so much. We often underestimate the attraction of knowledge. Men and women have sacrificed almost every pleasure in life in order to learn about areas that have no financial value for them at all, for example, religion, the occult, fine writing, and science fantasy. "Man desires to know" is perhaps the single factual universal statement we can make.

The fantasy life of the Teacher revolves around many mythical figures—figures that may, indeed, be historical personages, but are nevertheless mythical forms for the many. Some of these figures are Socrates, Aristotle, and Merlin, as well as Faust. Socrates claimed that he knew nothing, Aristotle was reputed to know everything that could be known, Merlin was a master of secret knowledge but was afraid of forces he could not control, and Faust sold his soul to the devil to acquire more knowledge and the power that it can give. Elements of these figures play in and out of the fantasy life of the person who elects the life scenario of the Teacher.

The images of Merlin and Faust contain genuine clues to the fantasy of the Teacher: the lure of status, of becoming awe-inspiring, of commanding power over other men and women. Merlin was the Henry Kissinger of the ancient myth. He ruled by giving advice to others, living as the power behind the throne. Faust was like the young German Ph.D.'s of the 1930's and '40's—the armed intellectual, the Nietzschean questor seeking to exercise power directly.

Such dreams have never been absent from the Teacher in any age. The checkered record of faculty fights through the centuries demonstrates that. The High Middle Ages saw wars between the schoolmen of Europe that rival the long history of war in Vietnam. Only in the past four decades have the intellectuals emerged to really exercise power in the political sense. From Roosevelt's crisis administrations until now, the professors have grown in power. The dream, however, was always there.

Immortality and the Teacher Scenario

In our fantasy life we teachers see ourselves as the rational parallel to the sacrifice of the Wounded Healer, the degree-bearing Christ figure. We will parlay the salvation we pass on to individual students (and at best to several thousand over a lifetime of teaching) to many millions, through our creative governmental decision-making, or, for some, through our inspired writings.

Each of us seems to have been born with the concept of our own immortality firmly in mind. Children, up to a certain age, find it hard to conceive of death as the end of a person. Many of us continue throughout life without really coming to grips philosophically with our own death. We act, and usually think, as if we were going to live forever. But the teacher, and the Teacher fantasy by which he or she lives, is usually not so naive. The Teacher may be an intellectual, and an intellectual is one who understands the limits put on human experience and power by physical death.

Indeed, beyond the lure of the material that may be learned, and beyond the unfolding of the flowers of the mind and the pleasure of the company of other intellectuals and students who are always young, it is the promise of immortality—through the twin pyramids of one's continuing influence on students, via the classroom, and on the history of ideas, via one's books—that exercises the strongest pull upon the Teacher. "To live in mankind is more than a name," the poet tells us. Indeed, it is; it is to live as an influence, as a power, as a veritable god whose genius is invoked whenever one's authority, insights, or theories are referred to by the passing cavalcade of human beings. It is surely preferable, to most people, to be remembered when one's upturned oar (in Homer's phrase) is seen than to be eternally forgotten. If death is a god, then achievements are gods, too. The Teacher, even when he misses the full exercise of power now, lives in the contented knowledge that his contributions may do more to shape the mix and flow of history than even the most map-changing statesman. In the fantasy life of the Teacher there is a general concern to triumph over death and the centuries to come. Intellectuals take the long view, dwelling on the underlying form, the inner nature of things. For centuries it was the only comfort they had.

The Magician

There are many professed teachers today and many who are not solely teachers but who live by the fantasy of the Teacher (for example, some soldiers, many ministers, business executives, writers, even farmers and carpenters), but there are not so many self-professed magicians. There are, however, many who live by the internal myth of the Magician, which is not far removed in dynamics and form from the inner story of the Wounded Healer or of the Teacher.

We live in an age of the revival of interest in the occult. History generally indicates that many men and women turn to occult subjects and practices whenever the foundations and certainties of their own civilization have been sorely shaken. Such is a good description of our time with its crisis of confidence in elected political leaders, the absence of adequate supplies of energy to fuel our greatly expanded economy, and the grim suspicion—put into words by the environmentalists—that we have passed the point of no return in our self-destructive poisoning of our

Earth. The Age of Aquarius, which dawned in the 1960's, seemed to peter out in unfulfilled promises in the 1970's, and turned mean in widespread fascination with William Peter Blatty's book and movie, *The Exorcist*. Suddenly there were more open, or suspected, magicians than we would have thought possible only a few years ago.

But nothing comes from nothing; nothing ever did. The wave of occult claims and supranaturalistic obsessions were not virginally born in the mid-1960's. The seeds of the occult revival lurked within the fantasy lives of millions, awaiting only a charismatic personality, a stimulating song, to be born. Such personalities, such songs emerged from the flux of experience. The rest is history.

What is the fantasy of the Magician? How does one who subscribes to this inner story see himself and the world? Not so differently from the Healer, for the Magician sees men and women who need help and salvation, too. Not so unlike the Teacher, also, for the Magician, too, sees a people who need guidance and instruction and a chance at some kind of immortality through the service of wisdom.

For the Magician, the reality of realities is power. The Magician's fantasy life is one of unbridled ego power. Oftentime, the Magician trespasses into the power of the id, into the instinctual realm. As in Faust's case—the Magician-Teacher—this may be more mistake than opportunity. The Magician's id is always active, to be sure, but only through indirection, through being taken up into, made malleable and directed by the ego. The Magician is basically intuitive but seeks to discipline even this intuition. The one part of the self against which the Magician always struggles is the superego. It is a struggle against the internalized restraints of civilization, one sometimes entered into by the Teacher, also.

The Magician's role is a tempting one. Every popular

magazine carries advertisements claiming to offer the secret of life, power over enemies and success in love. Magic's dark lure is as efficient today as it has ever been. But the inner egoism of the Magician's fantasy can be exercised in any area of life, even the most scientific. Anyone who seeks to manipulate the feelings, to play on the needs of others is subject to that *hubris*, that overreaching pride that can destroy both manipulated and manipulator. Ministers, priests, social workers, medical doctors, psychologists, and psychiatrists today are all vulnerable to the Magician's temptation.

The Wounded Healer works through the harnessed power of the id, and the Teacher through submission to the superego. The Magician is the master of the ego. On this analysis, most ministers (whose fantasies ought, by calling, to conform more to the Teacher's than to any other) are Magicians.

The Priest

The most universal of all quests, in fantasy life and in creative literature, is the quest for salvation, for the healing of all gaps in the self, for complete integration of all the life elements, for wholeness. This quest might easily be taken as the overall name for man's psychic life—and for his religious, artistic, and philosophical history. While all human beings drive toward some sort of salvation, some ecstatic moment of wholeness, either within the flow of life or at death, those persons in whom the quest has come to consciousness are living out, in heightened form, the inner fantasy of the Priest.

The Priest is the Wounded Healer conceived in the context of sacerdotal rather than healing forms; he is the Magician conceived as a mediator between God and man rather than as a conjurer of cosmic powers to aid ordinary men. The Priest fantasy functions under the life scenario element of the call—elected by God to be a go-between, an advocate of God with man, and man with God.

The Priest is, above all, a person of responsibility. He—or she, for there are countless women Priests—feels the weight of other people's groping search for the upward quest, and longs to help them. The Priest, though often concerned very much with his or her own salvation, sometimes is not consciously so; rather he or she is other-directed in either a loving or manipulative way. The Priest was not a popular symbol for much of the last three centuries and therefore the symbol was disguised in many fantasies. A pseudo-symbol, the social worker, arose in Western society, under which disguise people could live out the Priest's fantasies. In recent years the Priest has become much more popular, often highly respected. Today people can act out the Priest's life scenario with a clear conscience and a feeling of acceptance.

The Priest, in his fantasy life, and in exterior reality where possible, seeks to tap all three aspects of the self, id, ego, and superego, but with a view to subjecting the id to the ego, and both to the superego, conceived of under the high symbol of the Father God. The Magician manipulates, the Priest supplicates; the Teacher legislates, the Healer placates, conciliates, and affirms. In all, the drive to save the self and others, to come to wholeness and acceptance, is paramount.

Nothing said here is to be taken as implying that the life scenarios of the Priest, the Wounded Healer, the Teacher, or the Magician (usually) are not noble and ethical undertakings. Of course, the gap between the inner fantasy and the outer life style may be a profound one. There are

many more spoiled Priests in the realm of fantasy than
actual ones.

A female symbol of the Priest is the Nun, and it can also
be applied to many men. It is not often recognized that the
Wounded Healer/Teacher/Priest life scenarios trace back
to the mythical symbols of the old woman, the wise
woman, whose title was contracted into the "witch," and
the wise old man, even the fabulous old man of the
mountain.

The Christian Nun is not the archetype of sacred service
for women. Long before Christianity's rise there were
women judges of Israel, priestesses of Baal, Astarte, and
other deities. The temple prostitutes of Baalism, mentioned in the prophet Hosea's book, are striking examples
of peculiar female sacred archetypes. The king is always
accompanied by the queen, the priest by the priestess in
mythology. Mankind is a unity of male and female. Both
Jung in the twentieth century A.D. and Plato in the fourth
century B.C. observed that the unity was originally in one
person—the Androgyne or Hermaphrodite.

To say that the image of the Nun has eroded in popular
esteem during recent decades would be an understate-
ment. Hundreds of women have left the various orders,
although many orders have modernized themselves con-
siderably. The inner fantasy of being a Nun, a priestess of
God, has been displaced in many women toward the
pseudo-symbol of the social worker, and the fantasy of the
Teacher.

The Entertainer

In discussing the life scenario, the inner fantasy of the
Entertainer, we encounter a difficult problem—that of

separating the strong ego types who consciously develop themselves into professional entertainers, actors, comics, singers, and dancers from the insecure, weak-ego persons who fall into acting out an Entertainer fantasy at work or parties in order to attract peer group attention and approval. The professional entertainer and the Entertainer scenario are two different things, just as the academic philosopher and the cracker-barrel philosopher are vastly different types of personalities.

There are lots of silly people, as opposed to humorous people, but their number is not fixed; rather the number changes in size with the person who makes the judgment. Silliness is a matter of one's personal judgment, a question of opinion. Yet there is general agreement in small groups such as offices, schools, and neighborhoods, on the silliness of certain people, or at least of the so-called "fun-loving quality" of this or that person. In our masculine-dominated society the label "fun people" seems to be mainly attached to women, especially young and relatively status-less, attractive young women. To act silly, to become a "fun person" is, from my point of view, a revelation of a sense of social—and personal—inferiority. To be "fun to be with," in this sense, is a method of gross compensation, and, I would suggest, is less than fun for the person who adopts this style of social acceptance and survival.

Yet many people's inner fantasy life is one that turns around the elected life scenario of the Entertainer. One feels sympathetic towards entertainers, for in overcoming their inferior feelings, at least on the surface, these people add something positive—a little laughter—to the world. The problems arise because, on the one hand, the Entertainers themselves are not happy, and, on the other hand, they do not really increase the joy of well-balanced people, who do not need "Step 'n fetch it" type characters around them to feel comfortable.

One of the types of Savior-figures in all religions is the comic hero, the fool, the trickster, the clown. The riddler, or the prankster, is a mediator-type figure in both the medieval society of Europe (the Fool) and in West African religions. The Fool or the Trickster is one of the guises of the shaman. Tricking the evil spirits, and evil men, is no light calling. A fun person, today, may also dispell evil spirits, and bring some relief into tense human lives, so the circle may still be unbroken. It has never taken a completely healthy personality to be a helper of mankind in its need.

Looked at from the inside of an Entertainer fantasy, the world is a frightening, or at least, a tense and confusing place. He or she relates to this world by lightening the load of others through the evocation of smiles and laughter, and is then helped to cope with this world by those he has helped. The Entertainer is frightened by the world and never really learns to cope with it by himself, but he or she is not paralyzed by his fear and copes through a symbiotic relationship. Though not a parasite, the Entertainer does live off the surplus coping ability of others.

Inside, the Entertaining girl tells herself, "I'm so pretty," while recognizing that she really is accommodating. The number of such females who allow themselves to be taken advantage of is probably quite large. The male Entertainer may tell himself, "I'm so witty," but actually realizes he is merely outrageous and so diverting. "Harry is always good for a laugh," we say. We leave unsaid the common judgment, perhaps shared by Harry, that Harry is good for little else.

There is an element of the Entertainer in all of us. From time to time and in random areas of our personalities, and in varied aspects of social intercourse, we all feel inferior. When this dysfunction occurs many of us ease the bruise to our egos by joking, sarcasm, and laughter. Sometimes this kindness to the self is purchased by cruelty to others. Then the inadequacy of the Entertainer as a life scenario is revealed. Generations of ethnic groups who have been the butt of the Entertainer's "wit" bear witness to the brutality of certain forms of fun.

Sexual Aspects of the Entertainer Scenario

The Entertainer myth has diverged, in the mid-twentieth century, under the impress of the sexual revolution (or the revolution of rising sexual expectations) into a masculine and a feminine variant—the "satisfier" (or cocksman) and the "good lay" (or sexual playmate). These are human beings, who, in fantasy and in fact, see themselves as contributing to the human enterprise, chiefly in terms of sexual satisfaction. If there were not so much widespread sexual dissatisfaction, adult people would avoid such adolescent personalities, but under the conditions of present social existence they are generally welcomed.

The sexual entertainer, like the prostitute, can make a lot of social headway as long as he or she remains young and keeps his/her looks. Aging complicates matters. Alcohol and pills are generally relied upon then to take up the slack in the sexual entertainer's under-developed personality.

Such life fantasies, played out under cover of deception and darkness, have always formed part of the human story. Ours is only a more open, sexually honest age, like that of the Renaissance and the age of Elizabeth, so that we publicly acknowledge now what was formerly only privately recognized. The extent of our honesty can be measured by the social fact that the libido of millions has been liberated to the point of freeing their generalized sexual interest—therefore the huge volume of business in pornography, X-rated movies and slick, sex-oriented magazines. But the libido of these same masses is not free enough to carry them through this surface playing with sexuality to genuine freedom of total action. A similar comment might be made about the openness of lesbian and homosexual preferences. People talk about it, but there is a real question about their freedom to act out their verbal and lifestyle fantasies.

If the truth about human libido is actually that we are polymorphously perverse, then most of us are still where we always were, free in fantasy, and alone, but not so free in public or even in small groups. Finding the sexual revolution, beyond its preparatory bombardment of small talk, is a little like finding the Cheshire cat— it's all the shadow of a smile and not much claws, fur, and tail.

The Writer

Many ancient and not so ancient peoples did not write. Even when they did write in pictographs, things weren't spelled out in detail. The re-teller of stories had to use his imagination. It is said that the world would have lost many of the old stories if ethnologists hadn't written them down. Other great tales, like the epic of Gilgamesh, would not be known if archeologists hadn't dug them up and scholars hadn't translated them. Undoubtedly, we would be the poorer without these strange and edifying sagas. Musicologists have roamed the plains and the mountains recording the folk songs rapidly being forgotten by both red men and white men. Carlos Castañeda patiently sat for years, trying to remember all that Don Juan could tell him of the

way of the warrior.[10] Writers, it seems, have always been
the keepers of dreams, recorders of fantasies. But are they?
I sometimes wonder. As a writer, I have traveled many
strange roads as well as where there are no roads in this
world. Many folk who have befriended me not only were
not writers, they could not write at all. I have listened with
a glad heart even when I could understand little or nothing
of what they said.

Sitting in a front line observation post outside Andong,
South Korea, watching for the advancing enemy to reach
the river, I absorbed the myths of the Land of the Morning
Calm from the Korean soldier beside me. Chattering in
broken English, singing in quiet tones the "Ah De Dong,"
the pan-Korean hymn, love song, and national anthem
rolled into one, this illiterate boy taught me much as we
passed the time together.

Traveling from city to city in Japan, as a raw youth, I
learned to communicate by smiles and signs. Often, miles
away from post, I found myself beyond the help of any
English-speaking person, unable even to tell the "exit"
from the "entrance" sign on the train. I went to Japanese
movies, listened to Japanese songs. One movie I attended
turned out to be in French with Japanese subtitles.

I set out once, through Finland, from the bottom to the
top—from Helsinki, where English was spoken by some,
to the countryside, where Old Swedish was the language,
up north and through the forests, where that outlandish
Finnish tongue was the only currency, and finally to
Lapland where all speech was conducted in Lapp. Hand
gestures we all could understand; language we could not,
and nobody wrote anything down.

I love reading and writing, but the spoken word, the
myth recreated in front of my eyes by people who believe
and live the mythic fantasy—for that I have more than

love. In that mixture of word and blood and sweat, I have faith.

Writers often are born to just this faith and become writers as a way of attempting to preserve this shared life of the people, but there is no word strong enough to describe lived fantasy, acted myth, but life itself. Writers have preserved, have kept the dreams and fantasies alive, if only in books and in their hearts, when all others were forgetting the meaning of being human. This is the fantasy of writers, their inner story, their burden and glory.

But writers and writing itself, in that ironical and cross-purposed paradox that makes history live, have been the killers of the myth, the degraders of fantasy, too. Why would men want to write if they could remember? Why would men need to write if all could recall? Pious and habitual churchgoers need no prayer books, they sing the service out of themselves. No liturgical texts were needed to stage the Indian's rain dance or the war dance, though their complexity exceeds the most formal service Christians ever use. The minds and muscles of the Indians were thoroughly schooled in the chants, the turns, and the leaps of their sacred dances. Writing made technology possible, but in time it stunted and almost killed the fantasies that are the only human reasons for wanting to do or make anything. Only the word that grows out of the inner life and is shared with others in sweat and exertion, risk and adventure, hilarity and sorrow, dirt, grease, heat, cold, tears, pain, and blood is that Living Word which every natural ear from the beginning has been cocked to hear.

Perhaps writing down the innermost fantasies, the personal stories of men and women today is not a completely good thing. God forbid that people would abandon their own dreams for the fantasies written in a book. Let the reader beware.

The "I Can Do Anything" Scenario

Women's Liberation has been celebrated—and damned—in many forms and in many ways. One of the most outspoken celebrations of this long overdue bid for full freedom is the song, "I Am Woman," that contains the line, "I can do anything." When you are rising up from oppression, that is a good slogan to proclaim, to build up your own confidence as well as to put your oppressors on notice. When you are going to have to face wounds and death, it is a good thing to have "I can do anything" pounded into you also. That sentiment, in essence, is what our drill instructors drummed into us in Marine basic training. But like all forms of overcompensation, "I can do anything" is a fantasy. There are people who have inferiority complexes who may not deserve them, while there are others who are inferior in some ways and aren't aware of this. There are others with superiority complexes who don't deserve such self-evaluation either. We all have feet—or at least big toes and heels—of clay. As Martin E. Marty observes in *The Fire We Can Light*, sometimes we have "clay feet clear up to our navels."

"I can do anything" is a genuine life scenario for eternal optimists, exaggerated activists, high achievers and big, but cheerful, losers. "Situation possible" people are not numerous, but they are unmistakable when you meet them. They are the Aries of the Zodiac, the pioneers, the adventurers against all odds, natural leaders who, literally, don't consciously know fear. Without the men and women of this fantasy type it is doubtful that the human race would have survived, much less progressed so far. On the other hand, the Aries type (in reality, not just people born under the Aries sign) are few and far between because their survival rate isn't high. No one can really do everything, so somewhere along the line, a lion (who also doesn't know fear when hungry), a desert (that doesn't think at all), or the sheer force of numbers of other men bring such people down.

In exaggerated fashion, such a life scenario becomes megalomania, a kind of self-voted apotheosis. Alexander the Great is reported to have taken this road, and died mourning that there were no more worlds to conquer. If your vision is myopic enough, you can easily come to believe that. Antiochus Epiphanes (or Antiochus the Manifestation of God) ruled Syria in the third century B.C., when the Jews were seeking independence from Syria. Because of the sheer blasphemy of Antiochus' behavior, the Jews of that day named him "Epimanes," or "the madman." We have seen others in history with this same life fantasy. How else would we explain the attitude and actions of Adolf Hitler in 1944–45? Hitler felt that if he could not be victorious, then Germany ought to be completely, totally destroyed. He did all he could to go out in a genuine twilight of the gods.

Most "I can do anything" people aren't like that at all. They are not vicious, or even unprincipled, they are simply overly sure of themselves. It is this exaggerated certainty that causes the positive person trouble. He or she misses the weak points in thinking, doing, planning, and acting that turn up later and cause trouble. But more, the vast majority of people are just not that sure of themselves and consequently, the "I can do anything" person makes them uncomfortable and often threatened. Unity gives strength, so the threatened ones often combine to cause trouble for the positive one. "I can do anything" is a great life scenario if you like highs that are really high and lows that really hurt.

The "Number One" Scenario

Willy Loman summed up the all-pervasiveness, and the final demonic nature of the old middle-class American dream, in Arthur Miller's *Death of a Salesman*.[11] Done finally to death by his fruitless search for the financial and social success that he thought would redeem him, Willy crashes his car knowing he is worth more dead than alive. And yet his young son does not learn the lesson. Over Willy's grave he declares his allegiance to the same dream, to be number one. Willy's grandchildren are now with us, mingled in with smaller numbers of young people who have turned away from the "I can do anything" fantasy to seek a simpler life.[12]

In asking some state university students to write up brief (and anonymous) descriptions of their fantasies for me, I turned up many reports like the following:

"My fantasy story is to overcome the challenges presented to me. This rules my life, especially my life as an artist and a student. I want to do everything I do good, not for success, but for my personal satisfaction. I even want perfection in myself, in my personality. If my feelings are contrary to what I think they should be I must resolve the conflict and convince myself of the way I should be acting. I don't know that this is a fantasy, it's one of the motivating forces in my life, I think. I don't know whether I'm proud of it or upset with it, but it seems so ingrained that I can't throw it, maybe the whole thing is anti-itself, maybe it's a weakness and not a strength to always want to be great."

Another student said: "Since I was a young child I've listened to records, watched movies, and sang, pantomimed and acted while watching a mirror. I wished right then I could be an actress. I love to perform, hear applause, doing a good job. I lack confidence, talent and a voice to achieve my fantasy. I usually start thinking of this when I hear Barbra Streisand, or see a good movie. I've performed before in contests, school plays, etc., but in college I've quit performing so to speak. Now I act, perform while I work. Any place you're with people you can pretend to be on stage. Being a waitress in a nice place is performing—pleasing the customer, smiling and joking."

A young female student told me: "My Fantasy that is . . . way back in my mind is one that I'm trying to do away with. I reject it. I believe most females are stuck with the same fantasy, that of finding a wonderful, handsome, great husband and having a beautiful home to decorate with all the little knickknacks and having beautiful, intelligent, obedient children. I admit that I do resort to this dream when I'm down or depressed with what I'm trying to achieve.

"I want to be a very well educated person that gets more informed as years go on. I dream of being above a man. I want people to come to me for information. I want to be admired and well known.

"The fantasy about being a housewife is not building my ego, it puts someone else on top. I think I need to be number one, to build my ego." [13]

THE QUEST FOR THE PHILOSOPHER'S STONE, BASIC TO ALL LIFE SCENARIOS

The inner fantasy life of all of us is full of the dreams and ideals of the ages. As priests do their saving, healers their comforting, teachers their instructing, explorers their

discovering, and soldiers their adventuring, they are em-
powered as much by the drive to find and apply the
philosopher's stone, thereby discovering the medicine of
immortality, as they are by any social and rational
considerations. We move from place to place, time to time,
interest to interest, and person to person, asking in effect,
"Are you it?" "Do you have it?" "Is this the place?" "If
not me, who?" "If not now, when?"

Some thinkers have suggested that the quest for perfection is the inner drive of searching for death. The
French proverb that opines that sexual release is "the
little death" points in this same direction. An Irish poem
about the Irish soldiers who died serving overseas in
the British Army, from India to China, suggests
"Were there no graves in Ireland that you had to go
so far to fight and die?" *Eureka,* "I have found it,"
in legend and in fact, often does mean the final consum-
mation.

Modern scholarship differs from conventional wisdom
in that it states, on the basis of its investigations, that there
are no philosopher's stones, universal solvents, perpetual
motion machines and magical pills which turn water into
gas. The first law of thermodynamics is often quoted, as is
the second—with its pessimistic doctrine of maximum
entropy. But the inner fantasy life—even of the scientist—
is not so convinced as is his conscious mind. We dream,
and in our dreaming about the impossible often make it
possible and real.

With these slices of life, we have passed from the fantasy
of the Soldier of Fortune to "I want to be number one."
We are at the edge of things, where most of us are
today—in perplexity. But notice that there is nothing
either spiritual or sensual in these fantasies. The only

reference, even as a doubt, is to money and things. Somehow the lusty crusades of Genghis Khan strike me as more spiritual than most modern quests.

2

Changing Your Scenario

CHANGING OUR STORY

I have often thought that the essence of humanity is stubbornness. Human beings seek their own way and even cling to paths that lead to their own destruction just because they are *their* paths. Nowhere is this more clear than in the well-meaning attempts of others to make a person change his or her story. It is true that the mentally able person will change his story's plot only when he convinces himself—not when others force him—that he really wants to change.

There are any number of good reasons for wanting to change your story. Perhaps, as is quite likely, the story you are telling yourself is not really your story at all, but one laid on you by others—your parents or spouse or employer. To live by the plan that others expect of us is to resign to death in life. Young people strongly resist having another person's plans forced on them. I recall that the saddest person I have ever encountered was a mental patient in a Louisiana hospital who had absolutely no hopes, no desires, no plans, and no story to tell. Although she was conscious, in touch with reality in a rough sort of way, and able to speak, she could not communicate with me because she was not communicating with herself.

Sam Keen and Anne Valley Fox put the case beautifully in their little "how-to" book, *Telling Your Story*:

> To be a person is to have a story to tell. We become grounded in the present when we color in the outlines of the past and the future. Mythology can add perspective and excitement to your life. Within each of us there is a tribe with a complete cycle of legends and dances, songs to be sung. We were all born into rich mythical lives; we need only claim the stories that are our birthright.[1]

Annie Dillard, writing about herself in *Pilgrim at Tinker Creek*, remembers her childhood:

> When I was six or seven years old, growing up in Pittsburg, I used to take a precious penny of my own and hide it for someone else to find. . . . I was greatly excited . . . at the thought of the first lucky passer-by who would receive in this way, regardless of merit, a free gift from the universe.
> . . . I've been thinking about seeing. There are lots of things to see, unwrapped gifts and free surprises. The world is fairly studded and strewn with pennies cast broadside from a generous hand.[2]

Ms. Dillard has a very lively story going, in touch with her childhood, on the one hand, and as sophisticated as a Zen philosopher, on the other. But we are not all like that.

For all the information that the science of psychology gives us, I sometimes wonder why? For every one person like Annie Dillard or the ageless scholar, Roland Bainton, there are thousands who live in the classic state of quiet desperation. This despair, hopelessness, lack of enjoyment of life, and failure of purpose is most often attributed to the influence of others upon the wounded ones. Such beaten and often resentful people point to an early marriage, a large family, military service, economic deprivation, and dozens of other sound reasons why they find themselves where they are. They leave out only one element, that they have been telling themselves this story—or letting it be told to them—and are simply living out and freely accepting a role they have come to hate. Where there is life, a change of story is always possible. Such change, by no means, is guaranteed to lead one to happiness, but it will lead one to possibility. First, however, one must change his inner story.

I see the possibility of a change of story as the central fact of human life together, of history. Even ages and cultures that seem tremendously stable, with little change, had built-in mechanisms for needed changes in plot, character, and performance. The basic religious myths, with their cycle of birth, rebirth, marriage, confession, absolution, celebration, mourning, and death were vehicles of possible change for those who lived by them.

William Brandon, writing of the culture and history of the American Indians in *The Last Americans*, tells of Crazy Horse's response to the suicidal war provoked by white repression of the Ghost Dance:

Eight days after the battle with Crook, this camp was attacked on a Sunday afternoon by a regiment of Cavalry, the attack was defeated. Crazy Horse himself, shouting, "Today is a good day to fight, today is a good day to die," led a rush that cut off half the attacking forces. Every man in this surrounded group of Cavalrymen was killed in a desperate fight that lasted less than half an hour.

The attacking force had been the elite Seventh Cavalry . . . led by Lieutenant Colonel Custer, who died in the battle along with more than 260 of his men.[3]

For the Plains Indian warrior, as for millions of simple people in the tribal state all over the world and throughout history, every day was a good day to die—for, in their religious faith every day was a fresh start, a new possibility in their life story. Somehow, our industrialized, urbanized, computerized, and controlled society has lost the hearty appetite for creative change that characterized other societies that we consider relatively changeless.

The ironical secret of this conundrum is that in Crazy Horse's view, an individual could and did *change his own life story,* while society remained fairly changeless. In our experience, social relations, the means of production and transportation, government emphasis and communication media do change, while human beings attempt to "stand pat" in the midst of this whirlwind.

In Crazy Horse's world, a man could grow, running through the changes of his life, knowing that the tribe would hold constant, would always be there when support was needed. In our world, we hold fast to what we have, like the blinkered prisoners in Plato's myth of the cave,[4] and so stand still while the landscape is blown bare around us. Rapid social change robs us of security; refusal to change ourselves robs us of growth and novel experience, and thus ultimately, of happiness.[5] Too bad for us that Crazy Horse didn't win that last Indian War and dictate peace terms in the White House.

MARRIAGE AND DIVORCE

If each one of us is telling himself a story—and that story is the inner reason for everything we see, say, and do—then none of us wants our inner story disturbed by others, not even by God. To act in accord with our inner nature is freedom. That we so often conform to conventions does not mean that we do not do so freely. Our freedom consists in our ability to keep our story on the track, unfolding itself, much more than it consists in outer movement. For many human beings this area of the inner story is the only arena in which their thoughts count for something. Shunted aside by society, effectively disenfranchised by the confusion of politics, fearful of the worlds of finance and war, men and women have retreated again to the inner world which sheltered them in childhood and which, nightly, refreshes them in sleep.

Marriage can, paradoxically, either serve as a hothouse for the stimulation of this inner life, or become the most oppressive enemy of it. The proximity of the partner in marriage may break down the solitude and quietness needed to invest the inner story with energy and life. One may be forced to flee away into sleep to escape the probing eye and voice of the partner. Most unfortunate of all, the familiarity of marriage may expose the basic plot of one's inner story, of one's most private fantasy life, to the analytic mind of the other. Frankly, one way of understanding the acrimony that leads to divorce is the analogy of the broken story. One partner's intuition or deduction of the life story of the other partner is followed by a ridiculing or rejection of the script that the partner has fashioned for his or her life. Such a situation soon becomes intolerable, for this is more damaging, more threatening than the rejection of a person's publicly confessed faith. Here fantasy reveals itself as stronger than social convention, legal obligations, human "love," and sexual attraction. No one can live for long where his life story is known, unless it is in the context of full acceptance. To be known and to know are not unqualified good things. To be accepted and to accept is a superior—and happier—relationship. Accepting another's inner story and revealing your own to someone else is not easy. Over and over again people tell me that "at least I can communicate with my wife"—or husband. Some persons refuse all in-depth communication or else use such material to their own advantage, making further self-revelation impossible.

Friendships and dislikes are similarly based on intuition and shrewd guesses about "what a person is like inside." We have respect for those whose stories are compatible with ours. We do not like people whose inner stories seem foolish or immoral to us.

All else can be allowed to fall, but the inner fantasy life must go on. Unbounded by age, condition, health or any other circumstance, running forward even in dreams and during times of illness, a person becomes fully identified with his inner story. Not even death is suffered to interfere with this progress, as long as any psychic resources are left to combat the final disintegration. The desire to struggle against death as long as possible stems from the inner need to make a satisfactory end to our personal fantasy. As we shall see in Chapter 5, we want to complete the life story we have been telling ourselves all our life through. From this inner drive springs the movement to write letters, compose books and poetry, paint pictures, fashion statues, erect monuments, and write wills.

Theories of immortality figure prominently as projections of the inner stories of our personalities or individuality into an indefinite future. One man sees himself as a great inventor, another as a soldier of fortune, another as a priest or healer. Most women see themselves as beautiful and desirable, but today some women increasingly see themselves in roles formerly reserved for the male. Both men and women believe impossible things about themselves and the attempt to implement these beliefs is the outline of their lives and the stuff of our common history.

In our individuality, marriage, divorces, and impending deaths, we must learn to truly love one another by respecting the privacy of each other's inner stories, and in the security of our deepest relationships tell each other our own personal stories. Such a sharing is deeper than the communion of public worship, closer than the communion of sexuality—it is the ultimate unmasking in absolute trust. We must learn never to reject another's story, when it is opened to us, nor to pry into someone's fantasy life when they have not offered us free access to it. In such acceptance and respect we perform the holiest function one human being can perform for another—that of acceptance, or in common terms, of "mothering." In an age that is widely seeking for alternative forms of consciousness because it does not know how to expand the awareness of the consciousness we are, by nature, such a ceremony of acceptance or mothering may in future become the primary sacrament, a sacrament of united mind and feelings—of Spirit.

Modern people look nostalgically at the stories of past cultures, especially those of the American Indians, precisely because of the sharing of personal dreams, fantasies, and visions that characterized those cultures. We often speak today of the lost art of conversation, blaming television for the decay of intimate speech, but I see the overarching desire to maintain a public image, to come across as a successful person, as the real reason for the absence of personal sharing in our status-oriented world. The tragic career of Richard Milhous Nixon seems the classic example of this weakness in our time.

LIFE IN DEATH: THE WRONG PEG

Very few of us are subjected to Indian attacks these days, but many of us are the victims of a more exquisite form of suffering: a wretched marriage, a twisted relationship with a child, or a tormenting experience in employment. The legions of those who have been defeated by life are large, and their wounds are no less sore because they have defeated themselves. Internal mechanisms of self-destruction are as deadly as the plastic bombs of political terrorists. Bad marriages are constantly repeated, boring playbacks of scenarios neither partner enjoys.

Where there is little imagination on either side, such marriages can move along for years, or even a lifetime. A vague sense of unfulfillment, perhaps characterized by a free-floating depression or generalized hostility, might be the only symptom. Unfortunately, human beings are each unique in their makeup and few marriage partners are equally lacking in imagination and intelligence. The more aware, alert partner soon becomes dissatisfied. Once this point is reached, anything is possible, from desertion to violence. As morally reprehensible as these actions might be, they do represent real though ineffective attempts at changing one's life story. Even more reprehensible, from the standpoint of life itself, is the one who refuses to change at all. No one thinks the killing of Custer's troops was a good thing, yet few of us would condemn Crazy

Horse for defending his village. It is precisely this unconscious recognition that the deserter or murderer is not the
only sinner that makes the "triangle" such a popular novel
and movie plot. Few people in our society who have
enough interest to read or watch movies have difficulty in
identifying with the criminal. And it could all be avoided
by a change of story.

Harvey Cox reminds us of the medieval carnivals and
festivals of the fool in *The Feast of Fools*. Cox stresses the
need for relaxation, play, and a reversal of roles (change of
story) in human life. Letting it all hang out, letting go,
truly overcoming repressions is a characteristic of primitive societies, among European peasant cultures, soldiers
on leave, and college students in general. We middle-class
people don't ordinarily have the healthy experiences of
such a blowout. Perhaps we are so materially comfortable
that we are afraid we will be uncomfortable if we change.
We are something like the pigs in a slaughterhouse holding
pen; we may not like those frightening screams from
across the way, but we do like the food.

A science fiction writer once developed a story about a
man who went insane because he could hear the grass
screaming when it was cut. Few of us are sensitive enough
to hear the screams, silent or otherwise, of others. Some of
us cannot even hear the reality of our own selves crying
out, screaming for a change of our inner life story. Those
who do come wide awake, their inner ears filled with that
terrible signal, usually can hear the quiet crying of other
persons as well. When we are jerked awake, changed in
this way, we often adopt the scenario of the Twice-Born
Person.

You Must Be Born Again: The Myth
of the Twice-Born Person

Jesus spoke of the possibility of change in human life, using the symbol of rebirth. Nicodemus found Jesus' observations about a second birth baffling, according to John:

> Jesus answered him, "Truly, truly, I say to you, unless one is born anew, he cannot see the Kingdom of God." Nicodemus said to him, "How can a man be born when he is old? Can he enter a second time into his mother's womb and be born?" (John 3:3–4)

I have always wondered why Nicodemus was so perplexed, for the myth of rebirth is as old as human history and means far more than conversion from one sect to another. The second birth is a symbol for maturity, when maturity means an inward shift in the personal life story so that one is truly living his own life and not playing a role (being a "slave") laid down by others. Jesus used the second birth as a term for being overwhelmed by the call to follow the God within, instead of religious playacting through law-keeping and tradition-following. Nicodemus was old but not too old to finally start living his own fantasies, to grow up "in the likeness of Christ"—who was mature, honestly living his own story—and so find happiness.

The breakout from the boredom of life, the loneliness, the fear of death, to the emergence into community, into love, comes through the new birth—and this rebirth often comes through the holy days, the turning cycle of the mythic, religious year. It is through change, through holiday, through self-change and growth within the vehicles of play and worship and recreation, that one can be

reborn. The quest for God, the thirst for communion can
be fulfilled for the individual, at the person's own pace, in
a society where the mythic-religious year is central. The
ongoing recurring myths provide not only escape but
redemption from the ills of maladjusted personal relations,
and, in saving the individual, redeem society itself.

Somehow, New Year's Day just doesn't swing it.
Perhaps Easter could, if we could concentrate on the
ancient myth rather than on the Walt Disney-type traditions of chicks and bunnies and new Spring hats. If Easter
isn't a festival of rebirth, then there aren't any left.

The Twice Born are, above all, those human beings who
have experienced change not only in their exterior relations, but in the innermost recesses of their souls. These
people have a conscious appreciation of their inner story
because they have come to understand their earlier inner
story—which was not their own and therefore not satisfactory—and have undergone dramatic change to a more
agreeable one. In many cases they undergo the conversion
experience in respect to social and political ideas, which
has nothing directly to do with religion. In other cases, as
with St. Paul on the road to Damascus, Martin Luther in
his Wittenberg tower vision, or John Wesley at the
Moravian prayer meeting, the second birth is plainly
religious. In all cases, there is a general reorganization of
the person's life with a parallel releasing of powerful inner,
creative resources. The world is, indeed, shaped by the
Twice Born, from Moses to Mao Tse-tung.

WHAT WE REALLY WANT TO BE

All the world seems to be searching for self. "Who am
I?" is the question, among the middle class at least, of the

twentieth century. None of us feel ourselves to be the pure in heart of Jesus' approbation. We do not sense that we are full of light; we have not that will to do or be one thing that Soren Kierkegaard baptized "purity of heart." And so the charlatans arrived: all the witch doctors who will make us sensitive, sensual, image-aware, responsive, listeners, feelers, orgasmic personalities. We go from weekend to workshop to encounter group. I think we track the wind.

What self are we looking for? The self is a process, not a philosophical absolute. For what are we sensing, feeling, massaging, praying, meditating? Can it be anything else than to move from one phase of the self, as yet immature, to a future phase of the developing self, more comfortably, and wisely, matured?

I do not think much is gained by discovering the self. David Hume reflected upon his consciousness and found only thought, never the "I" of the self. It is like looking into the swirling butter churn and wondering where the cream and butter are. The cream has been destroyed but the butter is not yet formed. At bottom, the emerging self is such a fizzling, cloudy mess. Better to untangle the sounds put forth by the butter churn, the inner stories we tell ourselves as we spin, than to find only the froth of an unfinished self. Let us rather seek to discover what, at bottom, we would really want to become.

LIVELY SYMBOLS OF TODAY

Which symbols can we readily identify as being vibrantly alive in the late twentieth century? Is Christ on his cross still vital for many? Does Buddha under his Bohdi tree still attract those fleeing from the world? Is Prometheus still defiantly suffering at the bottom of our minds? Harvey Cox observes that liberal churchmen are symbol-blind, and he is largely correct. But we are living through a revival of interest in the symbolic foundations of religion today, and to remain symbol-blind is to invite religious irrelevancy. Men and women, the non-church-going as well as the churchgoers, are today recognizing the symbols that rise up into consciousness as they examine their inner life stories.

Major Symbols of Change: Death and Resurrection

One word above all others characterizes the slogans and doctrines of our time, the adjective "new." It may be that the more things change, the more they remain the same, but everyone seems to put faith in something new, even if it is a new return to old ways—as in the energy conservation and ecology movements.

No one wants to die, so immortality, involving disguises, is always a cheap belief to buy. The American way of death shows the fear of physical death most of us have. It is hard to believe in the resurrection of Christ, however, so men and women turn to more rationalistic hopes. One of these is the idea of reincarnation, the concept that the soul is not only immortal, but actually moves from life to life, throughout eternity. There is no need to believe in a scandalously unique resurrection-lord as such, since everyone is immortal. The number of movies, songs, and books based on reincarnation in the past five years is phenomenal. Mystery movies have presented stories in which the victim, murdered, returns to life in a new form and helps the police catch his own killer. Magazines run stories on the people who say they remember past lives. The unending cycle of death and rebirth is a very lively symbol for many today.

Reincarnation, with its long-term view of history, is directly opposed by the several symbols of the imminent eschatological event, the apocalyptic destruction of the world. These symbols are very real to millions, both within and without the Church, and seem to be increasing in power over the minds of young people. Rather than seeing the universe as endless time, into which the person will be inserted again and again, over and over as an active participant, the apocalyptic vision sees time as a line which originated at a higher point than it is at now, falling because of sin. This descending line, which had a beginning, also most definitely has an end—an end (believers tell us) which is coming soon. The number of people drawn today to the Fundamentalist theology of the imminent end is quite large and is still growing.

It is my conclusion that people who fix their inner fantasies on either the myth of the eternal return or on the myth of the imminent end (Apocalypticism) have abandoned their own personal inner stories, adopting some one else's "trip." Losing oneself in either the vast reaches of time or in the lure of a fast approaching end of things is really the loss of self. One or two steps more and these life scenarios might lead their followers into non-responsiveness to life, or in short, beyond fantasy into madness. Yet to live happily ever after, to experience the eternal in the now is not a madman's dream, it is the hope of every well-adjusted person.

Fools like me can never leave alone the inchoate feeling, the childhood assumption, the age-old myth of living happily ever after. Every fairy tale ends this way. The gospels also end this way, and so does Marx's prediction of the triumph of the proletariat and the withering away of the state. Choose your own myth—all mythologies seem to follow the same basic outline. For what other goal does the aged Mao struggle in his perpetual cultural revolution? Why do millions of Christians work, fast, pray, and give? There is nothing else to compare with this goal and this hope. There is nothing else. The drug addict seeks the perpetual high, the sensualist the eternal orgasm, the surfer the endless wave. Every writer hopes that his book, this book, will be the eternal book—revealing the depths of his unconscious, and so of all men's unconscious—and the summing up of every book that has, is, can, and will be written. Every real cook cooks as if his or her dish will be the central course at the marriage supper of the Lamb. In the name of mental health, how could it be otherwise? When a person loses that hope and dulls that edge of expectation then sickness ensues. A truly well person does live on tiptoe. Hope and hope alone is sufficient to awake us from sleep and put our feet on the floor morning after morning.

Freud has said that each of us has a deep-seated refusal to accept his or her own death. Yet hope and joy can never really come to life in us until we do accept our deaths, and move through that experience to a new life. Hope is not a cowardly flight from death but a courageous affirmation of life.

CHANGES IN FANTASIES, CHANGES IN LIFESTYLES

Today we hear much about lifestyles. We speak most often in the plural, of lifestyles, because we have come to realize that our freedom largely consists in choosing for ourselves just how we will live. People in every age group, from every region of the country, turn up living "mod," "beat," "hippie," "upper class," "jet set," "country," "Western," "Midwestern Gothic," and "professional" lifestyles. But I think that we overemphasize lifestyles at the expense of the heads on the people who live those lives. Before the act is the idea. Before the change of lifestyle there is the change of mind. The inner story is the foundation of the outward deed. Listen to the words the mouth is speaking, consider how the person approaches his work and casts his vote, before you pay too much regard to his or her lifestyle. The roots of life are within, as the button worn by well-dressed people a few years ago proclaimed: "I'm a hippie under these clothes."

Letters from the Inner World Dropped in the Streets

Our inner fantasies, our life scenarios often reveal themselves to us and others in our casual behavior. Perhaps the closest we can come to the central fantasy, the life-directing story, within ourselves and others, is in mutual partying or in the religious act of confession. Cartoonists and supersophisticates have poked fun at cocktail parties, teas, and coffee breaks for many years. Still we have them. Why? Because they are the secular equivalent of confession. For all the pseudo-intellectualism and sexual horseplay of the cocktail party, men and women do often unburden themselves to others at such affairs. The college beer bust, for all its hilarity, plays a similar role. We have been bombarded with testimonials to the fellowship-stimulation of marijuana smoking, so I will not add to that here. Since recent trends point to a revival of heavy beer drinking on campuses, along with pot smoking, perhaps we will have a revival of conversation in the next generation.

People who don't engage in play are precisely people who have attempted to repress their fantasy life. They have an outer life story—the dull, everyday professional or conformist lifestyle they follow—as well as a hidden story that frightens them when it expresses itself in dreams and in drunkenness. They seem to fear pleasure or the breakdown of decorum, for they are afraid of their repressed inner lives. Often such a stance in life leads to alcoholism or obesity. The Middle Ages acted with instinctive wisdom in setting up fairs and carnivals to give free range to vented inner feelings. A country where the fool cannot be king one day a year usually ends up ruled by fools 365 days a year. When you have to say, "Make no mistake about it, I am the President," maybe there *has* been a big mistake.

Another form of confession, the personal letter, often communicates more of one's inner story than formal literature. It is also often a more reliable source of historical understanding than the official record. We are told that the ancient kings of the Middle East falsified their public monuments, claiming victories they did not achieve. I wonder what these kings wrote to their closest advisors in private letters? Undoubtedly they also lied to their wives.

The New Journalism of today has taken over the techniques of fiction—the use of dialogue, anecdote, and fast-paced narrative—attempting to get closer to the inner story of men so that the inner story of society can be more fully revealed. The New Journalists have thus become the novelists of public events, the symbol interpreters of present experience, much more than the traditional newsmen or older novelists.

Men and women who deal in the realm of the imagination, creating fiction, are much more likely to recognize the overriding importance of the person's inner life in the choices the person makes and the deeds that he does. Novelists, even the most action-oriented or Marxist, are forced by their craft to see the pre-eminence of mind over action and lifestyle. "Things start here," the novelist seems to say, as he or she begins to reflect the thinking of the character. The "stream of consciousness" novelists in particular are the excavators of man's inner story. Our problems as readers with such men as Hermann Hesse, William Faulkner, John Steinbeck, and Ernest Hemingway, is that the streams of consciousness they imagine and record are "fresh from the box," still cast in the unbroken myths and symbols of their characters' inner lives. Such myths need interpretation. Symbols, though universal, are susceptible to private valuation. We need to know what the symbol means to this character in this time in this place.

Additionally, Hesse and Hemingway and all the rest weave parts of their own personal stories, their own assumed fictions into their works. What, after all, does the huge fish mean to Hemingway—a man who handled most of his personal troubles by going fishing and hunting? The fish may stand for the overwhelming responsibilities of life to the old man in *The Old Man and the Sea*, but the fish may be a symbol for "What the hell?" and escape from serious reflection for Hemingway and the rest of us. Occasionally we begin to suspect that the lifestyles of writers partly reflect their assumed fictions quite openly.

Most novels and fictional stories are not so much autobiographical as they are based on the personal fantasies of the author, on what he or she believes himself/herself truly to be. I have noted this acting out of inner fantasy in myself, particularly in my craving for adventure. One doesn't have to be a Zane Grey, a war correspondent, or a James Bond to have had multiple experiences outside the ordinary. Some have held that there is no such thing as ordinary experience, but only a series of unusual events that people melt down into the ordinary because of their lack of attention, courage, and intelligence. I rather think that that is true. When we begin to pay more attention to our inner fantasy life I believe we will also become more aware of the fantastic things that happen to us, if not daily, at least often. Why not try reflecting on your own experience in this light? You may be amazed at your own life experiences.

I tried doing this and came up with at least a few fantastic events in an otherwise "typically" middle-class life.

Fantasy in Everyday Life

I remember North Korea in November–December, 1950, a time that is never absent long from my innermost thoughts. I thought not of the extreme cold, fatigue, fear, or enemy mortar shells, but of the crazy soup my squad made out of the turkey carcass we saved from our air-dropped Thanksgiving dinner. In my mind's eye I can see an utterly fantastic scene which really happened. I can see dirty, bearded young men laughing and cursing, throwing gnawed-on turkey bones into a blackened ration can, stirring up the most unsanitary meal one can imagine. I can hear, with the ear of my memory, our noisy good spirits as we drank the soup—a party interrupted only when Chinese machine-gun fire literally tore the wall out of our tent. Perhaps it was sheer insanity, but it seemed then and still does seem like fun.

Life is the source of fantasy, and every element in every wild fantastic vision is extracted from the life experience of someone. I remember hitching a ride in the wee hours of the morning out of the desert area of Western Morelos State in Mexico. The truck driver and his helper made me and my companions lie down easily on top of their freight—a load of television picture tubes. We were happy to be off our feet and headed to town, bathed in the cool air created by the rushing truck. We almost burst with silent laughter when the truck was stopped by a military patrol—looking for dope smugglers. The driver whispered, "Keep quiet, try to look like Mexicans!" Since three of us were over six feet tall and all were fair-skinned, that struck us all as funny. But we managed to be silent and it worked. Our driver was so unnerved by this that he put us out at the first roadside *cantina* we came to after passing the roadblock. Who would have believed that a middle-aged university professor, his son, his brother, and a philosophy student could get into such a situation? Life is always fantastic if you are open to adventure, ready for all kinds of experiences. Such openness does not lead to happiness, but it is the very condition, the actual state of being happy.

Perhaps I'm a bit more adventurous than some, but I know there are millions like me. Most of us aren't Faulkners or Hemingways, but we do build our personal lifestyles upon our personal fantasies. Dennis Hopper, in making the film, *Easy Rider*, leads us to see that everyone is making a movie. That is precisely what I mean in speaking of our personal inner fantasies. Looking at our closest neighbors and at ourselves, we can see the truth of this. The more introverted character makes his movie by more or less excluding other people from the rehearsals in outer life. Like Walter Mitty his action goes on almost exclusively within. The generation of pot-smokers and dope-users is similar to this, dropping out of activities to enjoy the fantasies in their heads. The extroverted or aggressive personality, no less than the introvert, guides himself by his inner fantasy but seeks to involve others around him in his own movie. This is fine for the person who wants to be part of that movie, but difficult for the many people who do not like the plot. Domineering mothers, demanding teachers, and other such people try to drag us into their fantasies; often the only relief is escape.

THE INNER STORY VERSUS ROLE EXPECTATIONS

We still speak of most people as being conformists because the mass of mankind guides its life not by its own freely elected inner story but by a life script that has become a model for one particular social group. Conformity always means conformity to something, and in the mass this means a rather passive ideal that fits in well with all the other people that are playing variations on the same role. Obviously, when someone comes along who is in touch with his own inner life and is consciously or unconsciously living out his own personal inner fantasy, consternation results. The upsetting quality of the individual has never been so clearly presented in literature as in the real life experiences of Soren Kierkegaard. Consciously living out a rich inward life, Kierkegaard found himself at cross purposes with almost everyone in his society. Disdaining the life of a middle-class Danish intellectual, Kierkegaard deliberately lived out many fantasies in public, drawing the anger of church, press, and academy upon his head. Soren Kierkegaard deliberately played games with the conservatism of his society, taking private delight in the knowledge that his deeply spiritual inner story was not what the public thought it was.

In cinema, where the majority of people are willing to tolerate odd lifestyles and the outlandish behavior that results from following one's own inner life, we find mostly conformistic characters presented on the screen. Occasionally we see the odd man out or the life story of the self-realized individual, which is accepted by the public for the vicarious enjoyment it offers. When young people try to emulate these unusual characters, however, they are given short shrift by their parents or the law. James Dean is far more acceptable on late night television than he is as a lifestyle for teenagers.

A cartoon movie, produced in Czechoslovakia, puts the situation of the person living his own inner story very clearly. This short film is called *The Man Who Had to Sing*. It should be required viewing in every public school classroom at least once a year. A child is born, the joy of his parents, until he begins to produce the most awful humming sound. The parents try to get the noisy baby away, but not fast enough, for the neighbors try to kill the child. Somehow the child grows up to enter grade school, still humming or singing. The teacher tries to stop it, finds she cannot, and throws him out of school. The police counsel him kindly to stop and when he doesn't, they beat up his father. Still the boy does not stop singing. He is drafted into the army, where his constant singing brings on a physical attack by an officer. He still sings and the officer commits suicide to escape the noise. Returned to civilian life, he is involved in courtship and marriage, still sings and is thrown out of his house. He cannot keep a job because he must sing. Finally, the whole population of the city descends on him to physically stop his song. In a mystical experience, he escapes from them, rising higher and higher into the sky, until he becomes a star. In the closing frames of the cartoon, we see a coffin. Suddenly the lid rises and the little man pops up still singing, then slams the top shut.

The film makers seem to be saying that the person who is his own man, who listens to his own psyche, living out his own inner life story, will be odd and suspected by others. The reference to the rising from the dead leads me to believe that these Czechs are directly pointing to Jesus Christ in the only way they can, considering the Marxist ideology that controls their country. These people with cameras and cartoon pens have added another dimension to Alexander Solzhenitsyn's declaration that, "Man has distinguished himself from the animal world by thought and speech." And, they have added, "By the use of the camera and the pen and paint brush."

More than this, the little film forces us to see that our lives are movies, and that most of our movies are very dull indeed. They have forced us to recognize the truth most recently set forth by Karl Menninger in *Whatever Became of Sin?*—"they hang prophets".[6] The denunciation of Amos by the priest of the royal shrine, the imprisonment of Jeremiah in an abandoned well, the slaying of John the Baptist, and the crucifixion of Jesus Christ ought to demonstrate the extreme danger in singing a different song and refusing to stop. "It is expedient that one man die rather than have our whole people learn new songs—or start telling a different story."

KEYS, KEY, AND A KEY

We have all suffered from the pursuit of images—and consequently of loneliness—for so long that many remedies for this sad state of affairs have arisen in the past two decades. New psychologies barrage us on every side. We are parent-scripted, taped, debriefed, redirected, decompensated, dipped in hot baths—and somehow come out the other side the same old selves. What did we expect? The subject of our problem is, after all, ourselves. Once we tear the old grandfather clock to pieces, we are still stuck with it, only in a less useful and handy form. We have to live with ourselves until we die, and, if Christianity is correct, for a considerable period beyond that. Paying attention to our inner stories is a good way to make this life-long companionship more interesting and comfortable. If you would find the key to the human situation, your own or that of others, find out the inner fantasies that the individuals involved are trying to live out. There are many keys to man, but this is the key.

DREAMS: FANTASY IN THE BIBLE

Of late, it has become more acceptable to try to remember your dreams, record them, and discuss them with your friends. With the passing away of strictly doctrinaire Freudianism, dreams are increasingly seen as direct messages from the self and not as evidences of psycho-sexual maladjustment.

For Jung and Freud, dreams are manifestations of the unconscious. Jung observes in *Memories, Dreams, Reflections* that dreams are "compensations for the conscious attitude." [7] Freud had thought that a dream was a facade behind which its real meaning is hidden—a meaning known by the unconscious, but hidden from the conscious mind.[8] Jung disagreed, saying, "to me dreams are a part of nature, which harbors no intention to deceive, but expresses something as best it can, just as a plant grows or an animal seeks its food as best it can." [9] Jung later came to recognize that our dreams may be psychic defenses, warning us against the directions in which our thoughts are tending.[10] Carl Gustav Jung certainly took dreams seriously as there are 59 citations to dreams in the index to his autobiography!

Dreams are, in my viewpoint, announcements in symbolic form of the inner story we are telling ourselves. They are part of our inner fantasy life, but a part that, due to their nature of occurring in sleep, lie outside our conscious control. They speak, therefore, in pure symbol rather than through thought and words based on plot.

The Bible takes dreams very seriously, too. *Nelson's Complete Concordance of the Revised Standard Version Bible* lists 71 instances of the word "dream." [11] Dreams and dreaming get more space in the Bible than the assertion of revelation, which is what we might suspect, since men and women in both the Old and New Testament periods believed that God revealed his purposes to men, at least partly, in dreams.

Dream interpretation is formally called *oneiromancy.* Apparently both Jacob and Joseph in the Old Testament were very good at this. In dreams the people of the Old Testament saw indications from God of what the future would hold, as well as revelations of his will. In Genesis, Jacob's dream at Bethel gave him the inner confidence that ultimately he would be established as a great leader of his people.

Jacob's favorite child, Joseph, inherited his father's tendency to be in touch with his dreams. Genesis tells of two dreams Joseph had that foretold his rise to eminence in Egypt. Telling his brothers about these dreams caused

Joseph a good deal of trouble and he found himself a prisoner in Egypt. He secured his release from prison by interpreting the dreams of two fellow prisoners. Brought before Pharaoh and presented with Pharaoh's strange dream of fat cows eaten by lean cows, Joseph interpreted the dream in such a convincing fashion that he was made governor of Egypt. In Numbers there is a declaration that,

if there is a prophet among you, I the Lord make myself known to him in a vision, I speak with him in a dream. Not so with my servant Moses; he is entrusted with all my house. With him I speak mouth to mouth, clearly, and not in dark speech . . .

The Book of Job, on the other hand, makes light of dreams, using expressions like "he will fly away like a dream and not be found" (20:8). The author of Ecclesiastes is equally disdainful of dreams, saying, "for a dream comes with much business, and a fool's voice with many words" (5:3).

The great prophets do not make much of dreams. The popular interpretation of the prophets as those who foretold the future, is, of course, wrong. The idea of prophecy put out by sectarians and Fundamentalists has become very popular in recent years, causing great popularity for such exercises in fantasy as Hal Lindsey's books. Actually the prophets stressed what was happening in their own day and warned of what would logically happen in the near future. If social foolishness continued, then Israel could expect destruction. Their prophecy was no more a prediction of the future than was Winston Churchill's repeated warning about Hitler's Germany in World War

II. The announcement of the coming restoration of the people to happiness was done in the spirit of faith and hope, based on the prophet's belief in the nature of God. Indeed the prophet Isaiah (29:7) makes fun of dreams and visions.

Jeremiah 23:23ff. is a decisive passage in understanding the nature of prophecy. Here Jeremiah tells us that it is the false prophet that claims to have dreamed. God is reported to have said, "Let the prophet who has had a dream tell a dream, but let him who has my word speak my word faithfully. What has straw in common with wheat?" (Jer. 23:28).

The great prophets did not care for dreams because it is so easy for any dishonest or disturbed person to claim knowledge of God's will—or of the future—on the basis of a dream. One cannot share the experience of a dream with another, except in words during the waking period, so it is not possible to check up on a reported dream. The only dreams we can be sure of are our own. However, the patriarchal stories of the Old Testament are positive in their appreciation of dreams as is one of the latest books written, Daniel.

INNER FANTASIES AND OUR DREAMS

In counseling, teaching, and talking with all types of people in many areas of the world, I find that conscious attention to one's dreams is a characteristic, on the one hand, of those persons who have tried to develop their personalities and have become famous for their contributions to the world (i.e., philosophers, theologians, writers, psychiatrists, artists) and, on the other hand, of children and relatively uneducated people. The great mass of people in between, blue collar workers, white collar workers, and middle-class businessmen and professionals do not seem readily alert to their own dreams or the dreams of others. Women seem closer to their dreams than men, so much so that I consider men who are alert to their dreams (like Jacob and Joseph and Jung and Tillich)[12] to be men who have succeeded in developing their naturally feminine side (the *anima*) more fully than the average male. The reported attraction of these figures to women (and the animosity of men toward Jacob and Joseph) would seem to substantiate this insight. Jungian analysis aside, it may be that coming to terms with the opposite sexual element in one's personality is a process of dealing with one's fantasy life. Surely, one of the ways in which we come to grips with our inner life story is through attention to our dreams.

Dreams let us into the world of the unconscious, into the raw stuff of fantasy, beyond our conscious valuations of good and evil. As in the fairy tale world of myth, moral judgments on dreams do not hold true. As in Jesus' famous parable, the prodigal son wins out in fairy tales over the moralistic elder brother. Yet herein lies a great danger for the waking, conscious person. There is real evil in the world and it often breaks through from the instinctual basis of the emotional life. Nowhere do we see greater evidence of this instinctual, primitive pull than in the current vogue of occultism, symbolized by public interest in demonic possession and exorcism. The rise of this phenomenon demonstrates the recurring motifs of both men's dreams and the ancient myths. The Christian would be wise to oppose the fascination of these dark fantasies with a renewed dedication to that one who overcame death and the devil.

LIFESTYLE AS CLUE TO SHARED FANTASY

Traveling, as I have previously mentioned, does more than tire one, it makes one very observant. You notice and experience for yourself just how shared lifestyles often mean shared comradeship. To the degree that one is dressed appropriately (*i.e.,* in Marine greens, or faded blue dungarees and sandals, or a dark business suit), one finds his contacts ready-made.

At seventeen, cold and broke, covered with pimples, with a shaved head, I found myself hitch-hiking and bus-riding from Marine Recruit Depot to home to first duty station. If ever clothing bespoke the man, it was those ill-fitted fresh Marine greens. And how we young servicemen stuck together! Leathernecks and GI's greeted each other from afar at crossroads and in cafes. The marginal, the different, the set-apart from other men usually do recognize each other.

At nineteen, scarred by more than acne, limping and bitter, I spent the long trip home on a medical air evacuation aircraft in company only with those who had, like me, passed through the snow and fire of Korea. Even today, as a middle-aged liberal, I can understand why the gassed and wounded Hitler drifted to the beer halls, where the broken survivors of the 1914–18 trenches shared their company and their fantasies with their own kind. The most demonic personality has a human base. Shared experience and the life long fantasies—and instant replays—based upon it draw people together and are the bases of similar inner stories.

In foreign cities, the like gravitate to the like. It was true in war, and I have found it true in peace. The beads and the beards replaced the bandages and the badges, but the "hippies" of Copenhagen and the self-exiled Czech students in Vienna sitting on the iron pipe railings around St. Stephen's Dom showed the same characteristics we teenagers in the Korean War showed eighteen years earlier in Pusan, Seoul, Kobe, Osaka, Kyoto, and Tokyo.

Such comradeship rests as much on inner story as on appearance, for it is offered only to those whose uniforms are a true reflection of "where their heads are at." It was a shared experience, similar ideas, wounds caused by the same club of circumstance that made the comradeship real. A phony, a "hype," a play-actor cannot and does not enter the world of the shared lifestyle, for he does not share the same inner world as the decent, the real person.

Age, sex, color, lifestyle are surface things. Give me five minutes of conversation and I can tell where you are coming from, what your mind is like, what you really are; and you could do the same with me. If we don't pretend, if we are ourselves, if we are in touch with our own psyches and open towards others, we will have our acceptance. It is the outflowing of the inner spirit, beyond the combat ribbons and the peace symbols, beyond generation and education, that gives life and friendship.

If you would know the world through knowing other people, this is the secret: Get to know yourself. Don't be afraid to act out or tell your inner story—not what you consciously think you are, or what you think you ought to be, but what you really are inside. Getting your head together is more important than getting your possessions together before you leave home or before you get off the plane. Find out what you are into, let that be known in what you do and say, and get ready to shake hands with many different people in a variety of different ways.

3

Families of Fantasies and Religious Philosophies

"Pity this poor monster, man unkind not," a great poet, e. e. cummings, has written. But mankind does not deliberately want to be unkind. Unkindness comes about through those persons who are cut off from their own inner stories, who forcefully accept some dull, average story for themselves, and who then proceed to force the rest of us to live by it. The unkindest cut of all is the sudden realization that the person who makes slaves of others is a slave himself—to the ideal of slavery. This holds as true for the person who urges us to resist school bussing or the use of drugs as it does for the S.S. trooper who forces us into the ghetto—and then stays in the ghetto to watch us. The fellowship of the damned, the comradeship of the lost is not much of a fellowship at all.

The essence of the kindness that man wants to feel is expressed in the great families of fantasies we call the great philosophies and the great religions. Each private person in the Judaeo-Christian tradition reflects a similarity of inner viewpoints that enable us to speak of families of fantasies.

This familial theory is necessary on the basis of observation (people's fantasies tend to fall into recurring patterns) and of logic (there must be a finite number of personal fantasies, although the possible combinations of symbols may be mathematically infinite). I see the genuinely similar nature of many fantasies as a psychological basis of human cooperation. This includes the reality of common confessionalism among churches, common political ideas and a growing faith in the brotherhood of man taught by all the great religions.

COMPARATIVE RELIGION AND COMPARATIVE FANTASIES

Technical studies that seek to establish the similarities and differences between the major faiths are enlightening and interesting. Such studies often have far-ranging consequences, as in Arnold Toynbee's application of similarities between Christian and Buddhist "love" in his *The Study of History*.[1] These researches can also have practical effect as in the ecumenical movement. The amazing series of theological position papers on the ministry, the sacraments, and even on the papacy written by American Lutheran and Catholic scholars expressing the vast areas of agreement between these historically antithetical confessions demonstrate the value of such exact studies.[2]

The search for agreement goes on far beyond the traditional Christian church, however, in more difficult but possibly more important ways. Christians and Marxists have met together in fruitful dialogue in Germany and elsewhere.[3]

Christians and Buddhists have had discussions, from time to time, for a number of years. The late Paul Tillich went to Japan for dialogue with his Japanese Buddhist counterparts, holding discussions that caused him to alter the direction of his research and thought in his last years. The dialogue of Tillich and Mircea Eliade, of Systematic Theology with the History of Religions (1964–65), represents the high point of my intellectual life and the capstone of my doctoral studies. Tillich's book, *The Future of Religions*,[4] gives the gist of these exciting seminars.

Students of religion, like students of mythology, do find genuine similarities and correspondences between different faiths, which originated in varying parts of the world at remote times in history. The myths of Genesis, chapters 1–11, have parallels in almost all the religious systems of the world. Even the widely scattered American Indian tribes and bands of wandering Eskimos have flood stories, "arks" (or their equivalents, such as the back of a turtle), and etiologies (explanations) of why people fear snakes, speak different languages, and offer sacrifices to the gods. The common themes of the fairy tale and the sacred myth crop up everywhere, from India to Norway, from Alaska to Iran.

And the people within the differing yet similar great households of faith have inner life stories that are basically similar to those of others from around the world and from across the centuries. The "quest," that mystical journey of the hero (or the fool) to find the holy object, kill the dragon, or seek out the beautiful young woman, is found at every time and in every place. Rites of initiation and passage, of birth, death, and rebirth occur in all faiths.

"Unless a man die, he cannot really live" is a basic tenet of world religion.

These family resemblances between religions and cults are closest, of course, between people of the same race, nation, age, class, and experience. As such, these overlaps follow the kinship patterns observed and identified by anthropologists, but not necessarily so. As a young Marine visiting the vast temple complex in Kyoto, Japan, I breathed in a fragrance of incense that was new to me, but I could also sense the same human intensity and feel the same depth of belief that animated the stately Lutheranism of my childhood. I could easily see why Shinran, the Buddhist monk who taught salvation by faith in Buddha alone was called "the Japanese Martin Luther." The similarities of Buddhist abbots, priests, nuns, and monks to Roman Catholicism was even more profound. The bells rang and the candles flared and the liturgical chant went up in Japanese, which might well have been medieval Latin, for all I knew.

Many of us there, distraught, distracted, confused, physically, mentally, and spiritually hurt by the agony of being forced out of North Korea, found peace on these neat courts of gravel and carefully raked sand. "That which you worship as unknown, I declare to you," St. Paul observed long ago.

Reincarnation

> If the red slayer think he slays
> Or the slain think he is slain
> They know not the ways I keep
> And turn and pass again.[5]

Over a century ago, an American, a New Englander and

a Protestant parson, Ralph Waldo Emerson, wrote those lines dedicated to *karma,* the Hindu-Buddhist concept of the cosmic law of cause and effect. Jesus put our human, simple, popular apprehension of this universal law in these terms: "As a man sows, so shall he also reap." "Judge not lest you be judged." "Give, good measure, pressed down, . . . for the measure you give will be the measure you get back." The golden rule is based on this insight, an insight Jesus shared with thinkers in every world religion, from every time. "Do unto others as you would have them do unto you" was and is taught by American Indian sages, Confucian philosophers, Buddhist bonzes, Hindu gurus, Jewish rabbis, Catholic monastics, and Protestant sectarians. "What the world needs now is love, sweet love" is a universal belief, rather universally ignored.

Beliefs in reincarnation occur widely, too. Apparently originating independently as belief systems in India and Egypt, reincarnation, the faith in the ever-turning wheel of birth and death, spread all over the world. That, however, doesn't cover the subject, since well-developed beliefs in reincarnation are found in Alaska among both American Indian and Eskimo groups. The belief that death somehow cannot really touch us is very widespread, as Freud was aware.

The pan-communal doctrine of reincarnation is growing, spreading wider and deeper throughout Europe and America. The rising tide of serious interest in occult topics and beliefs has been largely accompanied by some acceptance of the tenets of reincarnation. This presents a real problem to Jewish and Christian theology and religious practices. The cyclical view of history and the gentle though solid cynicism of Ecclesiastes, that there is nothing new under the sun, is growing and contributing to the development of a conservative quietism in America.

I have talked with many people, most of them young, but some quite old, who are Western believers in reincarnation. Their fantasy lives are very rich and, in some cases, would qualify as mentally "odd" by psychoanalytic standards. Dreams, visions, states of regression to "previous lives" under hypnosis are reported. In teaching university level courses on Eastern religions and seminars on the occult, I have encountered many cases like these. I feel that everyone who talks this way does not necessarily take the subject too seriously, but many do. The imagination knows no bounds, nor is it likely that it has any.

Personal life stories of "reincarnationalists" (to coin a word) differ from the reported inner life stories of the rest of us in the Judaeo-Christian tradition. The sense of building up to climax or of steadily moving toward a life denouement, with fulfillment at death, is missing. The effects of *karma*—or of carryover tasks and tendencies from other lives—is pronounced. The frame of the self-picture of one's own life has been pushed outward, and continues to expand, leaving the present scene less sharply defined, fuzzier and less packed with demand and tension. "Reincarnationalism" brings with it a kind of cosmic peace, a levity and decrease of "seriousness" about the world in the present that strangely contrasts with our common-sense Western approach to life. While the mountains of decision and challenge are leveled down, the valleys of despair and hopelessness are filled in, too. The piety of endless time is a measured and a quiet piety.

East and West

The East, in the guise of *karma* and karate, Zen and the sitar has almost overwhelmingly invaded the popular culture in North America and elsewhere. Toynbee was not the first to attempt to synthesize the higher religious insight of the East with that of the West. He will not be the last. But I do not believe that this conscious, philosophical effort at syncretism, at the mutual harmonization of Eastern and Western worldviews will finally succeed. I think there is a great gulf fixed, not of truth or morality necessarily, but of consciousness, between the basic religious outlooks of Eastern and Western man. I do not think that a Westerner can genuinely be a Buddhist. By the same token, it may not be possible for an Easterner to be a Christian, in the Western Roman Catholic and Protestant sense, either. Membership—especially when one is self-elected or brought in by means of an emotional experience—is not the same as participation.

To truly belong to a family of faith, one must participate, one must grow psychically out of a tradition. Converts are always the most harsh persecutors of non-believers, the most frequent in attendance at worship, the most committed, because they are, in Eric Hoffer's words, "true believers." True believers are not participants in the living body of the faith. Their fantasy lives, their inner stories were laid down, were fully formed, before they met the new theophany, before they were struck blind and given new eyes by the new Lord. The religion of the true believer is only technically, creedally, confessionally—in the outward sense—the true religion. The shared experiences of birth, life, marriage, death, and hope (or fear) of eternity are the essential elements of the true faith. Eastern or Western, a Jewish ex-student or a Protestant ex-truck driver dressed in saffron robes, with shaved head, and psychologically "high" on chanting the Lotus Sutra is, at base, a non-practicing Jew and a lapsed Protestant. The church has not always baptized infants for nothing. There is more to Jesus' saying about accepting the kingdom as a little child than a boost for humility and trust. We become what we are. We live out our own inner life story, and we receive the elements of that story, plot and plan and participants, from the faith and culture which gave us birth. Genuine individuality can never be drowned in the amorphous sea of generalities that characterize present-day popular religion. This is why the converted Saul/Paul was still paying his Jewish vows in the Jerusalem temple when he was arrested. And that is why I found that I could pray at the great shrine at Kamakura, but only to Jehovah, not to Buddha. The mercy the Westerner wants is more life, not escape from life into nothingness.

More Light Means More Life

The Westerner, in general, does not mean to depreciate life when he decries life's problems. The Westerner, on the average, does not want to die, for he finds life rewarding. In America our call is for more life, not less. The philosopher Goethe on his death bed called for "more light." He meant more consciousness, more life.

The Buddhist ideal of escape from individual consciousness is profoundly antithetical to the Western psyche. We want heightened consciousness, in fact, several modes of alternative consciousness, in one lifetime. This search for more—in experience, in life—explains not only our acquisitiveness and materialism but also our penchant for alcohol and drugs. The Westerner, particularly the educated Westerner, really wants to live many lives, all at once, right now. "Stoned again," the college students say. "Drunk by nine," the middle-class businessman admits. In the space of a day we change our mode of consciousness several times. We might agree that it would be cool, a real "rush," to be a Buddhist, but we would want to be "straight," to be sober, by morning.

If the Eastern philosophical mode is one of increasing quality, of diving down to the roots of experience, sloughing off previous usages and needs, then the Western mode is one of increasing quantity, of adding one to one to one—until the sheer bulk of things possessed and events experienced gives birth to a new quality of relations. Therefore the American consumes such a great percentage of the world's resources, and uses so much of its energy in travel and in holding back the night with artificial lighting. One car won't do, two cars are needed, then three. Not one house, but two houses, with trips to motels and rented beach houses in the summer. Add more to more and you have it all. I think our inner lives know better.

The little things looked at from our mainstream middle-class culture, trip us up. Romance, adventure, excitement, danger (yes, even danger)—all the things that the movies and TV series present vicariously to us, but which Disneyland and even the Playboy Club do not actually deliver—these elements stir in our subconscious and disturb our waking lives.

A FAMILY OF FANTASIES

Just as religions show family resemblances, so do the myths and interior dreams of people all over the world. No family of fantasies is more compact, similar, and universally understandable than the set of symbols about sex and adventure.

One of the most common dreams of adventure among

Americans involves some escapade in the Wild West, perhaps crossing the desert with little water and less food, or living for a while in an Indian village, unable to communicate except by smiles and hand-signs.

Why is such an adventure so appealing? Is it because of its connection with Indians? The psychoanalyst Carl G. Jung once said that he never undertook an analysis of an American that did not show up a streak of the Indian in his psyche. I think that is true. Rightly or wrongly the American Indian is fixed in our unconscious as the symbol of freedom. This appears to be true in American history from the earliest colonial days until now. Huck Finn and Tom Sawyer always expressed the desire to be free by thinking of running away, either to become pirates or to join the Indians. It isn't a bad dream. All commentators agree that there were few "type A" heart-attack prone people among the Native Americans. They lived free, even though often miserably poor, because they were free inside.

Often men dream of Indians. It is amazing how many of the Spiritualists, who go into trances seeking to know the other side of death, speak of meeting "Indian guides." Our culture, which destroyed Indian society and came close to exterminating the Indian peoples, has seen the Indian as a higher spiritual type for many years. Indians figure prominently in our literature, music, and art. How difficult it would be to imagine Hollywood without the figure of the Indian! I don't think I ever saw a full-length feature at the movies before I was twelve that didn't revolve around cowboys and Indians. As a typical young man, I refused to see *Snow White*—although I secretly regretted it. Getting out of knickers into long pants was tough enough without sissy movies.

The Indian turns up in our dreams. Perhaps the

Spiritualists do meet the wise old sage who speaks of Wakan Tonka, the Great Spirit, but the rest of us probably see the Indian of the Great Plains, dressed for battle or for flight upon his fleet-footed pony. He symbolizes for us that economical, aesthetically clean adventurer striking for the main chance, for freedom and happiness, without the unnecessary responsibility of house and car and insurance and security. His riches are worn on his back, his security is the lance in his hand, his social relations are blazoned in the feathers and beadwork of his dress—announcing the secret society of warriors that is his profession and his religion. His character is in his face and he needs no identification card, nor purse, nor extra coat and shoes to traverse a pitiless land. He lays up no treasure for tomorrow beyond the treasure of experience and the acceptance of his friends. His introduction is not by title but by the recounting of brave deeds, and his inner thoughts dwell constantly upon the poetry of his self-chosen death song. What if he is cold or struck blind by the sun? Or that his belly is shrunken with hunger and his lifestyle is full of pain? That is why we are not all American Indians, why I sleep in a bed a score of times for every time beside a campfire. Our dreams show us that we wish we were Indians, but our bodies cry out "No."

The lure of freedom gleams and glistens as the darkness falls over us in sleep. For a moment the inner story that lies so near the mystery that is our life takes over. And then we wake. It isn't a bad dream.

The Borders of our Mind

Architecture, at its best, and sometimes even at its worst, reflects the myths and symbols, the inner life stories of both the people who build the structures and those who use them. Keep this in mind when you view the coldly precise and purely functional modern skyscrapers of New York and Chicago. Think of it as you see the pseudo-Spanish architecture of Florida.

But most of all, think of the border towns you have read about or visited—stateline towns between Kentucky and Ohio or South Carolina and North Carolina, and true border towns like Brownsville-Matamoros and McAllen-Renosa in Texas and Mexico. Borders, the artificial dividing lines men draw on a map, are ecstatic, psychically-charged places, where the inhibitors of the superego are weakened in many persons. The landscape begins to take on an exteriority that is a better reflection of our inner stories, in such "boundary-situations," than it does in our character-armored subdivisions in middle-American towns. In these border towns there are fewer churches, schools, food stores, veterinary hospitals and Masonic halls; there are multitudes of bars, dance halls with obscene dancers and dances, liquor stores (at cut-rate prices), shops selling erotic items, cigarettes without taxes, and heroic though tasteless art. Swords, whips, non-working firearms for hanging in your den, ash trays with sexual and scatological symbols painted on them—the things we repress in ourselves at home all flourish openly here, just across the border. This is not hyperbole, but what I have seen in a lifetime of travel. Border towns (except for the communist side in East-West frontier situations) show most of these phenomena, and more. In many such places today, soft and hard drugs are readily available. On the U.S. side, the last sign you see as you leave the border is a warning not to bring any marijuana back, on penalty of five years imprisonment, if caught.

Recently I traveled to all quarters of our country on a university lecture tour. One trip took me to the Rio

Grande Valley of Texas. I took the opportunity to visit Mexico and crossed over to Renosa, in Tamaulipas state, on both of the days I was in the area. I was struck by the concrete confirmation of my thesis when I observed that the red light district (called "Boys' Town") was the area of Renosa nearest to the border. All you had to do was cross the bridge and make a turn, and down the street you would find the caustic excrudescence of America's repressed sexuality. Driving through in the daytime, when everything was closed and the fulfillers of fantasy were enjoying their hard-earned rest, I received dumbfounded stares from the *policia*. Nobody goes there until after dark.

This law of city planning holds true in border towns everywhere. The "Zona Roja," the red light districts of the world, may soon be found only "on the boundary." Men—black, yellow, red, white, brown—are everywhere alike.

Sacred Fantasies: The Acted Parable

A reading of the minor prophets Hosea and Amos in the Old Testament, along with the major prophets Isaiah and Jeremiah, reveals the rich inner fantasy life of the religious personality. The creative imagination of these men, revealed in their sacred fantasies or acted parables, was immense. Hosea imagined the state of Israel to be a faithless wife who degenerated from adultery to public prostitution. In order to illustrate Israel's faithlessness in regard to Yahweh, the Lord, Hosea married a woman, Gomer, who had been a harlot. Hosea had children by Gomer, and then forgave her of her sins, redeeming her even from the auction block of slavery to illustrate the Lord's forgiving mercy. Hosea translated his sacred fantasy into an acted parable of sacramental grace, of overwhelming religious and ethical power.

Amos' sacred fantasy life ran to seeing Israel as a basket of overripe fruit that was beginning to decay. He could visualize Israel as a masonry wall that had been built out of "true" and was being measured by God with a mason's plumbline. Amos fantasized (correctly) that the Master Builder was about to tear down this ill-founded wall.

That great and evidently princely prophet we call the First Isaiah became a "streaker" because of his sacred fantasies. He literally ran through Jerusalem naked to show the captives' fate that awaited a faithless and unjust people. Isaiah performed this nude parable not once but many times, going naked and barefoot for three years.

One thing has grown in intensity in my mind as I have grown older in a life filled with experiences with all kinds of people, everywhere—that myths and symbols are real, the most real kind of reality there is. The language of religion, of myth is the purest form of truth. Sacred fantasies and acted parables are not comments upon life, they are the roots of human life themselves. What is in our minds is not an attenuated form of reality; only what is processed by and interpreted by our minds is reality. Our young people who struggle to "get their heads straight" and handle reality are right.

Jeremiah knew this truth about fantasies and parables, as did Hosea, Amos, and the First Isaiah, as well as Dietrich Bonhoeffer, Paul Tillich, Emil Brunner, Karl Barth, and Rudolf Bultmann. Jesus certainly knew this truth, which is why he spoke in parables, despite what the Evangelist had to say about this (Luke 8:9–10).

Azmuth to Aztec

Everyone who is interested in history—and most of us are—knows that history deals with symbols. It is fitting that mankind is so bound up with history, for history is the blending of symbols into story. While history proper begins with man's monuments and written records, surely humanity has been telling one story out of many stories for tens of thousands of years. The images and symbols of our inner life, which Jung called "archetypes," may indeed be the mental residue of that great story of birth, growth, development, decay, and death. Literature, the remembered word, is our true treasure, embracing poetry, drama, history, and scripture. Lying in his prison cell, John Bunyan told his own story while telling the story of a pilgrim to his tablet, and through that to the world. In seminary I studied with a man who kept his Bible by him in a Nazi concentration camp, poring over its every word. He so impressed one of the officers that the officer arranged things so that the man survived. We live by the word, both by the inner word we tell ourselves and by the outer word by which God and the human race address us.

In 1950, I sat behind the hulk of a destroyed fishing boat on the banks of the Han River, peering over it from time to time to watch the city of Seoul being razed by the sixteen-inch shells of an American battleship, the artillery of the First Marine Division, and the rockets fired by F4U Corsair aircraft. I only looked up occasionally because I was reading an Armed Forces edition of H. G. Wells' *War of the Worlds*. Literature has power to obliterate the absurdity of the present moment and to give us the insight to live for the future.

Man lives by the recurring symbols of his common story, the symbols found on monuments and in literature.

In Morelos state, Mexico, my son and I climbed up an Aztec pyramid with a farmer we met at the foot of the mountain. Darkness was falling and we were edging along near the top trying to make out the carved reliefs in the stone. Suddenly we saw one clear figure in the stone, a peon in a procession. He was wearing a sombrero exactly like the one our guide had on. The centuries that stretched between the two figures, one stone, one living, suddenly collapsed into each other. I no longer had a sense of history as one-thing-after-another but as an ever-living story. The literature of the pyramid—and it was a work of literature as well as of architecture—was immediately made real by the living symbol of a simple, but enduring, sombrero.

The Sacraments

Sacred fantasies and acted parables are still part of our ordinary religious life. The ordinances of God's house, the liturgies and rituals of worship ranging from the Greek Orthodox to the Southern Baptists, all enshrine the insights of the creative imagination. But nowhere are sacred fantasies and acted parables more clearly presented than in the sacraments. In baptism we believe that we die with Christ to the world and its powers and are raised again to newness of life, even as Christ rose from the dead. The sacred fantasy is still there, still powerful, whether the means of death to the world's power is represented by three drops or 100 gallons of water. "I baptize thee in the Name of the Father and of the Son and of the Holy Spirit"—the words spoken are as effective in Catholic ritual as they are in the more literalistic expression of immersion in a Kentucky river. St. Augustine once sagely remarked that baptism could be performed with sand if no water were available. I have always liked the Texas joke that tells of a drought so bad that the Baptists had to sprinkle and the Methodists used a damp cloth in their services.

The sacred fantasies and the acted parables of the Old and New Testaments show their common psychic origin with the civic, ritualistic dramas of the ancient Greeks and the elaborate religious dances of the American Indians and Polynesians. In the acted parable of the Lord's Supper we are in the presence of drama, presented in myth and symbol, as well as in the elevated words of moral exhortation. Before conscience there was feeling, before commandments there were signs. In Jesus' ritualistic restructuring of the Passover meal there is a deepening of values, a return behind commandments to signs, beyond conscience to feelings—in the wholistic sense of cognition and affection, and not just of sentiment. Nowhere is Jesus' fantasy power better expressed than in this daring appropriation for himself of the place of the sacrificed lamb on the Paschal table. "This is my Body," Jesus declared. "This is my Blood." What startled faces must have greeted that announcement! But the power of his inner story was so great that each one in his turn bit the brittle bread and drank the pungent cup, seeing in the outward sign the inner reality. At every Communion service those who truly commune enter again into that pregnant fantasy of 2,000 years duration, knowing through feelings beyond words that Christ is there.

The creative imagination of the Christian sacraments is often overlooked through our habitual use of them. To many church members they are just "old fashioned" practices. We miss the existential depths, the sacred fantasies of broad scope that make them up. There are few experiences in life more packed with fantastic meaning:

To die and rise again with your God and to eat the very flesh and drink the blood of your God is a far-out idea. The rationalism that has eaten away the nerve and meaning of biblical faith in the Reformed and Free churches obscures what the Mexican peasant still knows: the tender turning up of the very tissue and marrow of psychic life in these observances.

St. Paul puts the matter simply:

> Do you not know that all of us who have been baptized into Christ Jesus were baptized into his death? We were buried therefore with him by baptism unto death, so that as Christ was raised from the dead by the glory of the Father, we too might walk in newness of life. (Rom. 6:3–4)

And:

> For if we have been united with him in a death like his, we shall certainly be united with him in a resurrection like his. (Romans 6:5)

By the same tokens, the Lord's Supper is an acted parable expressing the most far-fetched (and fetching) sacred fantasies. Shouting theologically at the Corinthian Christians who participated unfeelingly in this rite, Paul declares:

> When you meet together it is not the Lord's Supper that you eat. For in eating, each one goes ahead with his own meal, and one is hungry and another is drunk. What! Do you not have houses to eat and drink in? Or do you despise the church of God and humiliate those who have nothing? What shall I say to you? (I Cor. 11:20–22)

And again:

Whoever, therefore, eats the bread or drinks the cup of the Lord in an unworthy manner will be guilty of profaning the body and blood of the Lord. Let a man examine himself, and so eat of the bread and drink of the cup. For any one who eats and drinks without discerning the body eats and drinks judgment upon himself. That is why many of you are weak and ill, and some have died. (I Cor. 11:27-30)

Quite an imagination! Failure to utilize the religious imagination is here said to produce illness and death, as well as unlovely factionalism. The sacred mysteries, acted out in sacred fantasies and parables, have power.

Ernest Hemingway found it difficult to believe, but his long experience in Italy, Cuba, and Spain led him to value the Roman Catholic faith. He was moved by the ritual of the Mass, the sacred processions and the sacral fantasies of the simple people he knew who prayed to and through the saints and who clung to the mysteries of the faith even when war, natural disaster, and poverty made mincemeat of their lives. One day in a Latin American cathedral will give any open-minded person the same experience. Perhaps it isn't too fantastic to suggest that a church ought to be a place where people can go to pray.

I have seen the same simple faith among Protestants. One of the most moving experiences of my life, repeated many times, has been the Lutheran Communion Service. One of the most meaningful acted parables I have ever participated in is the loving washing of feet among Protestant sectarians, the Winebrennerians. This simple ritual still has power to bring forgiveness and forbearance into play in the hectic lives of twentieth-century people. The fantasy activity of serving one another, of humble participation of leaders and led, of younger and older, of clergy and laity is the basis for that kind of community we all inwardly seek. But its power must come from within, growing from the depths of personally participated sacred fantasies, from shared living with the gospel story. Done as a sign, a mere convention of membership, the rite rings hollow and evokes laughter, not tears.

Sacred Fantasies of the Bible

The Bible is a great reservoir of materials for the fantasy and imagination. Not only Ezekiel and Daniel or the Revelation but the gospels themselves are the sources of creative visions and ever-new ideas.

In reading the gospels everyone conjures up a picture of Jesus himself. This is quite in line with the emphasis in Jesus' preaching that held that we should use our God-given minds for ourselves. When Jesus told the parable of the different types of soil, which is in effect a long and involved Oriental fantasy, his best friends and oldest followers confessed confusion. Going up to Jesus after his sermon they asked: "Master, will you please explain this parable to us? People asked us what you mean and we did not know what to tell them!" St. Matthew (13:34) editorializes, "All this Jesus said to the crowds in parables; indeed he said nothing to them without a parable." Yet when the disciples asked, Jesus readily explained his meaning to them. "Ask and it shall be given to you," seems to have been Jesus' motto in a lot of things.

In another place Jesus reacted against the disciples' thick-headedness, saying, "If I have told you earthly things and you do not believe, how can you believe if I tell you heavenly things?" (John 3:12). The point of this explanation of the parable of the weeds of the field (Matt. 13:18–30) is that the disciples, though morally earnest men, religiously inclined, did not exercise their religious imagination very much. Jesus was a storyteller who gloried in spinning tales that made people laugh, cry—and most of all—think. Jesus particularly tried to drive people beyond thinking to help them come in contact with their own psyches. Jesus was himself in close touch with his own psyche, and functioned with his emotions "out front," in the parlance of our day. This is why Jesus often became angry, wept, embraced people, simply got up and walked away, and in general "knew what was in people's hearts." Our teenagers would say that Jesus picked up the vibrations of people around him.

Jesus was a full-orbed teacher, in touch with the depths of his own personality, unashamed of expressing his own emotions and eliciting the emotional response of his audience. Because he spoke from the depths of his own inner life, exposing his inner fantasies in ways that other men were not capable of doing, he differed significantly from the moralistic and rationalistic scribes who served the Pharasaic community. This brought the recognition of the crowds that " he spoke as one with authority and not as the scribes" (Matt. 7:29). Nothing was too fantastic for Jesus to use in his teaching. We recognize in his style the mark of the creative thinker, of the artist and philosopher who thinks in structural, concrete terms. Jesus looked and made a correlation between weeds and men, between types of soil and types of human inner lives, whereas others looked at a field and saw only weeds among the wheat. The stony ground Jesus identified with closed and selfish hearts, and this image took on the colors of a portrait in Jesus' mind when he talked about such cynical persons. Rich soil Jesus saw as loving, ever-growing inner persons, and he compared the fertile soil of the Judean countryside with men of big hearts. Jesus' mental health and intelligence is signaled by the leaping, creative fancy of the inner life revealed through his conversation.

Only in our lifetime have churchmen and educators come to recognize the play of fantasy in Jesus' work. Only recently have we begun to recognize the vital role that imagination plays in the mental and spiritual development of human beings. Numerous commentators tell us that we must stop fearing the minds we have and learn to trust that which wells up from the center of our beings. Mankind's imagination, the source of all creativity and the birthplace of all that is new, is the nearest link the creature has with his Creator. The One who spoke and made earth and sea and light and man has imagination!

Portrait of Jesus

Every generation has read the gospel story of Jesus and, perhaps unknown to itself, come up with a portrait of Jesus interpreted through the prevailing imagination of the times. We are familiar with the Anglo-Saxon portraits of Christ that were popular from the Victorian period to the 1940's. Here the Jew has become a middle-class North European. I have in my library a little book, privately published during the years when the Beat Generation was popular, which declares that Jesus was a beatnik.[6] Albert Schweitzer has made very clear this generational distortion of Jesus into the prevailing outlook of the times in his famous book, *The Quest for the Historical Jesus.*[7] Subjectively oriented writers made Jesus very subjective, rationalistic writers made him a rationalist. Theologians influenced by Kant made Jesus a moralist. Here the religious imagination was at work, but it was out of control, for it was not recognized as such. Rather these imaginary reconstructions were thought to be the result of objective, scientific research. The same might be said for the more recent modern quests for the historical Jesus.

The old Russian Orthodox Church exercised much imagination in its approach to scripture. Highly valuing the monastic life of self-denial and putting a religious value on suffering, a legend arose that Jesus was crippled and deformed. Because of this legend, which held that one of Jesus' legs was shorter than the other, we have the famous Orthodox cross which has a downward tilting bar at the base of the cross.

There is a scriptural basis for the rise of this legend. In Isaiah 52–53, we read about the Suffering Servant, whom Christian thought has identified with the Messiah. The text says:

As many were astonished at him—his appearance was so marred, beyond human semblance, and his form beyond that of the sons of men . . . (Is. 52:14).

And again:

. . . he had no form or comeliness that we should look at him, and no beauty that we should desire him. He was despised and rejected by men, a man of sorrows, and acquainted with grief; and as one from whom men hide their faces he was despised, and we esteemed him not. (Is. 53:2b–3).

The context of the Servant songs shows that someone, either a personification of the people of Israel, or a prophet, or in the orthodox Christian view the Messiah who was to come, was of a very ugly, even deformed appearance and was further tortured and crippled before being put to death. At least the old-time Orthodox were realistic enough to know that Jesus could have been the Christ and still have been ugly and ill-formed. At any rate, this is a clear example of how the religious imagination works with ideas that are highly valued in a culture and so develops theology and ritual.

TORTURED FANTASIES

Not everything that comes up from the inner fantasy life is healthy. Every pastoral counselor, clinical psychologist, and psychiatrist is familiar with religious obsession. Mental wards are full of patients for whom religion is a burden, not a means to liberation. Milton Rokeach has detailed a story of three men who believed themselves to be divine in *The Three Christs of Ypsilanti.*[8] Popular literature and movies reflect public awareness that there are some tortured souls who believe that they are Napoleon or Julius Caesar or the Virgin Mary or Jesus Christ or God. Such people really exist, although there are many more who labor under the delusion that they have been called to be prophets, to announce a new commandment or to foretell the end of the world. Mental wards contain many of these while many others are operating freely in society, converting other disturbed minds to believe in their peculiar visions. The problem here is that the essentially fantastic nature of what these people proclaim is not recognized by their followers, who take these dreams literally.

The destructive power of the imagination enters human life when one does not recognize imagination as imagination. Literalistic biblical preaching, particularly on texts taken from Ezekiel, Daniel, and the Revelation, tend to take on the color of schizophrenia. Indeed, such preaching produces schizophrenic reactions in personalities that already are marginal in their hold on reality. I have had occasion to interview a number of such persons.

My friends on the psychological and psychiatric staffs of a medical center where I attended seminars for several years used to delight in introducing me to their patients with religious obsessions. Of course, both they and I knew that arguing theology with such persons is useless. This is exactly what Rokeach found in his Ypsilanti study. Rokeach attempted to break three men, all of whom thought they were Christ or God, of their delusions by bringing them together. He felt that their conflicting claims might push them out of their delusions and bring them back to reality. Unfortunately, schizophrenia does not work that way. The three people were able to accommodate their mutually exclusive claims and recognize each other as God, or else explain away the others' claims as being the work of insane men.

There is nothing more frustrating than discussing the tortured religious fantasies of such people with them. Everything turns in a circle and nothing changes.

In one veterans' hospital I talked at length with a man who had been hospitalized on and off for more than twenty years. He felt that he had been called as a new prophet of God. He was otherwise harmless, although he could not hold a job since he disturbed fellow workers, with his evangelistic activity. His wife would keep turning him in to the hospital after he spent all his money preparing letters to mail to clergymen. Every clergyman knows about these letters, since most of us receive at least one a month from someone. In talking with this man, I found that he had no new religious ideas, indeed, few disturbed people do. What sets them apart is the typical feeling of a personal calling to preach a new law or gospel, which gives them a sense of great personal importance. Such disturbed people will stick to this "call" regardless of their lack of personal qualification for such tasks. A total failure to convince others of the truth of their message does not stop these "called ones," for they know the prophets were rejected.

Recently, I lectured to some medical college students on various religious and psychological matters and afterwards, true to form, my hosts took me to visit several mental institutions. The doctors introduced me to patients tortured with religious fantasies that had brought them to the point of such non-effectiveness in living that they were committed to hospital by the courts.

One young woman in particular had been victimized by obsessive thoughts about the death of Christ for several years. When I saw her she had just undergone a series of electric shock therapy treatments. Electric shock is not as horrible as it sounds, for only a mild electric current is introduced to the patient for a very short time. Psychiatrists are not precisely sure just how electric shock therapy works, whether it breaks up conscious thought patterns by its shock effect, or destroys some of the basic electrical-chemical neural pathways in the brain, or whether it simply causes obsessive ideas to be repressed into the unconscious portion of the brain. That the treatment works is without doubt. This young woman at first had difficulty in remembering just what her religious fantasy was when the psychiatrist asked her to describe it to me. At first she had to say, "I'm not really sure," although just a few days before, this fantasy had driven her into a state of nervous depression.

The young woman's fantasy revolved around the passage in the Passion Story which says: "It was now about the sixth hour, and there was darkness over the whole land until the ninth hour, while the sun's light failed; and the curtain of the temple was torn in two." (Luke 23:44-45). The usual interpretation of this passage is an optimistic one, for it is taken to mean that the dividing wall of separation, of sin, has been removed from its blocking position between God and man. The patient, however, interpreted it as a literal symbol of judgment on her, that she was to be torn in two (either physically, psychically, or by the separation of the spirit from the body; she was not clear), and consequently, took the death of Christ as a judgment of doom upon herself rather than as a basis for the good news of salvation in Christ.

This person seemed so calm after the electric shock therapy, and the attending psychiatrist seemed so interested in having me discuss religion with her, that I did discuss the Passion Story with her for a while. I already knew that it does no good to discuss religion with people with fixed ideas. I pointed out to her the historical setting of this symbolic passage. The Jewish temple was so arranged that within the holy place there was a Holy of Holies, separated from the rest of the temple by a veil or curtain. Only once a year after an elaborate ritual of purification was this Holy of Holies entered, and then only by the high priest, who sought to pray for the forgiveness of his own sins and the sins of the people. A Roman general at the time of the overthrow of Jerusalem sought to profane this spot by entering it and was shocked to find that it contained no images or furniture, but was completely empty. The Jews, of course, believed in the invisible presence of God, who could not be represented by idols.

According to the early Christian theology that underlies the writing of the gospel accounts, Christ's death superseded the temple with its sacrifices and the Jewish high priest's once-a-year prayer for atonement. Christ was the true high priest, so that the elaborate priestly ritual had come to an end. This is the symbolism behind the tearing of the curtain in two; the Hebrew high priest's function was ended. Henceforth men who believed in Christ had immediate access to God through their faith in Christ.

I tried to point out that this was a hopeful, promising text. The young woman said she could understand what I was saying but she could not feel it. She could only feel the judgment she deserved that made this text a promise that the splitting of her personality, which had already begun in life, would be completely carried out at death. She observed that she had deduced her interpretation of the condemning function of Christ's death from the teaching of her Baptist congregation in East Texas. It seemed that each time that she went to church her obsession grew stronger. She had been brought back to the mental ward so many times after attending church that her psychiatrist had ordered her not to go to church, although he was an elder in the Presbyterian Church himself.

SUMMING UP

In considering personal fantasies, families of fantasies, and the great religions of mankind we have observed that continuing human social groups, from nations to religions to philosophical and political groups, are based on shared story similarities. Not only communities that share a mythological heritage—like the ancient Romans who called milepost zero in the center of their city the *umbilicus* or center of the world—but faiths, communions, sects, and political persuasions grow out of shared inner life experiences. If we do not share a similar inner fantasy life and spend our lifetime telling ourselves the same kind of personal stories, we can hardly be genuine co-believers with other people.

Many of our problems in the modern world have arisen when we have failed to recognize inner life fantasies for what they are. We have often taken fantasies common to our generation and community as objectively true descriptions of how the world is. Sometimes the prevailing fantasies of the time are identified with the assured results of science. Carlos Castañeda has reminded us that every apprehension of reality, including that shored up by the supposed findings of physics and other disciplines, is still only an interpretation; it is still only what we *imagine* the world to be.[9]

In considering some of the tortured people that our society and our religion (like every society and every religion) have produced, we have been made aware that all fantasy and imagination is not an unmixed blessing. Our fantasy life, like our body, can become diseased. And like the body, the test of the healthiness of the imagination is the test of the fruits of the process. An imagination which makes for unhappiness and pain is no longer creative and free. An imagination that sees the world as hostile and alien or a fantasy that makes one uncomfortable is not healthy—and needs a physican.

PERSONAL FANTASIES AND LITERATURE

Our family fantasies, the basic religious philosophies into which we are born become our own when we appropriate them for ourselves and incorporate them into a personal fantasy of our own. Such a personal fantasy may then become the basis for stories or works of art in creative men and women.

A person may go along for years wondering what his life is all about, trying out one fantasy after the other and still feeling dissatisfied. This trying out of various life stories is perfectly natural in childhood and youth and even through college. At least in former times little boys dreamed of being everything from railroad engineers to astronauts. Most of them ended up working in offices. The following is an account by an American writer of how he found out what he wanted to do with his life in a moment that the theologian Paul Tillich would have called one of "ecstatic revelation." His whole life changed and he found the beginnings of what would be his inner story.

I once bought an abandoned farm with the intention of remodeling the barn and reviving the farmyard. Although the house had been built in pioneer days, there was a sense of its having been lived in during a more recent yesterday, for at least a dozen families had left their marks. The barn, on the other hand, gave a feeling of never having been changed since the time it was raised.

One night when I was wondering what the original builder might have been doing at the same hour two centuries ago, I chose to think he most likely would have been putting his stock to bed. So, trying to recapture something of the past, I walked toward the old barn. Feeling like a ghost contemplating the business of haunting—there was indeed a powerful sense of another time—I breathed in the winter freshness of the night and felt that I was reliving some certain moment. I could smell the musty tang of hay and manure, and it was easy to imagine a restlessness of farm animals within the barn. I pushed open the half-collapsed door and stepped into the blackness.

At once, I seemed to have an overwhelming sense of satisfaction and safeness: there was a welcome softness of hay underfoot, and although they could not be seen, the surrounding walls and the oversize beams made themselves felt, almost like something alive there in the darkness. The incense of seasoned wood and the perfume of dry hay mingled to create that distinctive fragrance which only an ancient barn possesses. I felt a strong affinity for the man who had built this barn. Perhaps some of his reverence passed on to me—perhaps that instant was the beginning of my regard and affection for old barns. It takes only an instant for a person to be directed to a path that he will follow for the rest of his life.[10]

All of us live by our inner fantasies, we all work at the unravelling of our life's inner story, whether we are aware of it or not. Some of us are more in touch with our psyches, with our unconscious selves, than others. Among human beings who commune most with their unconscious, who are more interiorized—and more developed in fantasy awareness than the average—are surely poets, writers, and dramatists. Ironically, writers are also among the best observers of the activities of others, gauging the motivations and inner life of other people on the basis of their awareness of their own self-processes. This inner life coupled with active and shrewd external evaluation is the mark of poet, novelist, playwright, and non-fiction writer as well. It is a full-orbed, more fully developed way of life than the intense preoccupation of the introvert with self or the thoughtless response to external cues of the other-directed person or extrovert. Indeed, poetry may be the purest human mode of being in the world, since in poetry one attempts to cast the most inward sensations of subjectivity into words designed to communicate not only comprehension of data but apprehension of feelings and one's reactions to the experiences of life. Poetry evokes the total range of human response, knowledge of, feelings of, and wonder at the world we inhabit. In poetry the medium is the message and the message is the medium.

LIFE SCENARIOS AND LITERATURE

Readers and critics have often accused writers of producing autobiographies, either more or less disguised. Many writers have not defended the objectivity of their authorship because they have actually written autobiography. A writer like T. S. Eliot, whose work shows a wrestling with the crisis of faith after World War I and during the great world depression, gives credence to the belief that the writer writes about himself. Eliot's conversion to Anglo-Catholicism, reflected in his poetry and plays, tends to confirm this thesis.

I would like to hypothesize that the writer does, indeed, often write about himself. One can only write about what one has experienced, observed, or fantasized, in any case. An author writes, after all, from where he is, from the worldview, the *Weltanschauung* or philosophical position he has so far attained. Writers are interesting persons, to themselves first, and later, if accepted by the public or a portion of it, to other people too. But generally writers do not only produce manuscripts that offer a situation report on what point they have reached in the unfolding of their own inner life story. That fact is reflected in their work, but it stands behind, often deeply hidden in the books, plays, movies, and poems they create. In a work of art or scholarship, the creative person also reports on what he has seen, sees now, and envisions for the future. An author's works and a painter's paintings are always a little ahead of themselves. Works of art have an integrity, a purpose and projection of future trends of their own, apart from the creator himself or herself. The unconscious mind leaks out a roadmap of where the author is going that often amazes no one as much as the writer himself. "The moving finger writes and having writ moves on, nor all your piety or wit can rub out half a line of it." Creation is a transcendental, a trans-personal act.

Literature develops, is written, and functions at several levels. Writers have a way of including wish fulfillment in their material—of writing about what they would like to be (but are not yet, and may never be), all from a conscious, ego-directed level. This strand of posturing, of mock-romantics and pseudo-heroism, must be disentangled from the leaked announcements of where the unconscious self proposes to go. In the struggle of destiny (the real coalition of the results of free choices and social, biological, and psychic determinism) with loudly proclaimed liberty, destiny always wins.

Let us examine some classic and modern stories for clues to the life scenarios they exemplify.

Crime and Punishment

"When you sup with the devil, you must use a long spoon," an old proverb tells us. The young student Raskolnikov forgets that warning. Dostoyevsky delineates the internalization of Nietzsche's "Higher Man" (*Übermensch*) concept, of the person whose mental development has placed him "beyond good and evil" in this story of pride, sin, love, and repentance. In genuine fashion this is the explication of a man's inner fantasy life and of his translation of it into concrete reality. Moving through the work is the counter-theme, the counter-fantasy of Christianity: the virtue of humility, the preciousness of every human life, and the self-defeating nature of evil. *Crime and Punishment* is a parable that yields meaning at many levels. It might be taken as a warning against the egoism of Western intellectualism and its trust in logic and science. Don't forget the sanctity of every life, it tells us. It certainly is a warning against the self-deceit of master race theories, whether held by eccentric German or Russian intellectuals or by lower-class Bohemian National Socialists—or white Americans and South Africans.

Raskolnikov decides that he can morally kill the old pawnbroker to secure funds to stay in school. His future usefulness to society outweighs the old woman's claim on life, he believes. Unfortunately, he also finds it necessary to murder the pawnbroker's innocent sister. The student slips the axe inside his coat and gets safely away. From then on, his conscience does everything it can to turn him into the police—and finally succeeds.

"Wither shall I flee from thy spirit? If I make my bed in hell, thou art there. . . ."

Raskolnikov is pushed over the line to confession by his evaluation of the self-sacrifice of Sonia. Sonia loves her useless father and her brothers and sisters so much that she sells herself to support them. At first despising Sonia, the proud intellectual comes to fall at her feet, seeing in her the suffering love symbolized in the passion of Christ. Raskolnikov confesses, is sentenced to Siberia, and has his redemption confirmed in Sonia's decision to go to Siberia also, to wait for his release.[11]

Dostoyevsky has given us a story not only of crime and punishment, but also of conversion and redemption. Here is a graphic description of the Christian doctrine of *Agape,* clothed in flesh and history by the creative imagination of one man. This is not Dostoyevsky's story alone, but a re-telling of a culture-wide myth, the story of Christ, here reincarnate in the figure of Sonia. Raskolnikov is Saul become Paul after sacking the churches at Damascus, for the blinding vision and the turning around of life is the same. The myth of that heroic conversion, that "turn-around" or *metanoia,* lies deep in our literature and social life.

The Unvanquished

The Unvanquished is great writing and good reading, and more, it is a conscious part of a series of works explicating one sensitive person's vision of how his region got the way it is, and where it is tending. Where is Faulkner in this story? Is he the young boy playing war in the dirt of the front yard as the story opens? Surely there is some of Faulkner in him. Through this boy's eyes, ears, and mind we are introduced to the racist society of the Deep South at the turn of the century. Through him we are delivered over to the culture myth of the American white (of all sections): the firm yet inchoate belief that the Other, the marginal man, the oppressed, whether Indian or Negro, has reservoirs of wisdom and strength not possessed by the White person—powers possessed because the Other is in touch with his unconscious, his primal self, and through that with the dimension of spirit.

This book is opened to us, and with it the inner psychic and outer social worlds of Faulkner's region, through the inner life fantasies of one young boy. In him we see the centuries-old dread of the master race: that the victims are the unvanquished, that the inferior are the superior, unconquered by superior knowledge and physical power because they are protected from corruption through continued communion with the inner world. It is Faulkner's key fantasy that this unspoken dread is true. The old aristocracy is crumbling; soon it is gone. What replaces it in the land of white power?—the Snopes, the rising businessmen who are the manipulators of technology and the purveyors of desired goods and services. As Carlyle remarked, "Those who desire cheap goods are at the mercy of those who seek to provide them." Cut off from black emotion, cut off from the intellect and taste which the ante-bellum gentry put in its place, we are delivered to the free enterprisers, the spiritual leaders of the cotton gin, the Ford franchise, and the savings bank. In time they will bring forth those monuments of the new culture, the taco chain, Walt Disney World, and the Holiday Inn.

Faulkner, of course, writes about himself, but also about thirty-five million other people in his time and place. Faulkner writes what he feels inside, surveying just how far his own inner story—and the longer story of his family—has come. But he also writes of what he observes, he tells us the way things have been.

Faulkner's greatest legacy is the delineation of his characters. The old Negress in *The Unvanquished* without social status or legal recognition is nonetheless (or precisely because of that) a redeeming figure. The fallacy of racism (or of moralism in general) is that it is the most needed parts of our selves, as well as our own evils, that are projected on the other and so pushed away. The figure of the white man standing on the Negro, trying to keep him down—to repress him—is psychoanalytically correct. Faulkner, both as writer and as character element in this and other novels, comes across as a wounded healer, the shaman who has wrestled with the demons, won a totem-badge, and limps through the pages of his books showing us the power of our evil spirits.[12]

Reflection

It is said that some read to think, some to prime themselves for writing, and some for entertainment. The first class of readers is rare, the second common, and the third form the great majority of the reading public. This observation holds true of those who converse, travel, and have an interest in their fellowmen. Some have only the simple and natural human interest in learning all they can about others and just enjoying their company. This was—and is—the lifestyle of many countercultural people from the Beat generation through the hippie generation to the "plain person" generation of today. Young people with whom I talked in doing *The New Mentality*[13] could never understand why I would want to write about their lifestyle rather than just live it.

Others desire information and seek the company of strangers out of curiosity, or even out of a sense of superiority. I do not think the writer falls into this category. The writer is one who is vividly aware of his own inner fantasy life. Faulkner shows this, as a Southerner, throughout the bulk of his work. John Steinbeck, the chronicle-keeper of the dispossessed during the Depression, was close to those he wrote about in *The Grapes of Wrath, Cannery Row,* and *Of Mice and Men.* Herman Hesse's deepest inner life story, with fantasies of the most profound sort, was involved in *Steppenwolf, Demian,* and *Magister Ludi: The Glass Bead Game.*

Hesse's personal fantasy seems to have been one of becoming wise in the wisdom of the East as well as of the West—a fantasy which eventually failed. Hesse's profoundly sad story of the man who thought himself to be a wolf of the steppes apparently tells us that seeking wisdom may not be the happiest story we can tell ourselves. The wolf is known to us only through his notebooks. His life seems desperately unhappy. At the end of *The Glass Bead Game*,[14] the Master finally frees himself from the pursuit of wisdom to attempt to simply live. He drowns on the first day of his retirement. The Master had deferred human pleasures and the development of his fantasy life since childhood. He had sublimated his innermost needs, drives, and desires. In the height of his powers, he resigned his administrative post and headed for the relaxed life of a tutor. Rising early, the Master and a pupil dove into a mountain lake for a pre-breakfast swim. Only the pupil came out. The future seemed bright and fresh, but it was in short supply.

Hesse is saying that one day may not be enough to finish telling ourselves the story we have so wanted to tell ourselves all through our lives. It is later than you think.

The younger generation of the 1960's and early 1970's picked up on Hesse's journey to the East in a big way. Rock bands were named for his works, and the Glass Bead Game became widely known as a parable for our society. Hesse stimulates the mind, leading us to see the high stakes involved in the decisions we make. To seek to know who we are and how things are, spiritually, is an attractive lure.

Like Hesse, André Malraux shows modern people some sense of what they could be but have failed to realize. Hesse points to wisdom, Malraux to the greatness people fail to recognize in themselves. In *Man's Fate*,[15] Malraux attempts, using the techniques of modern cinema, to give people a sense of the grandeur they have missed in themselves. Malraux shows a life fantasy of the Soldier of Fortune type, stressing the brotherhood of those drawn to desperate causes. He seems to be saying, be careful of the story you tell yourself for you will find yourself having to die for it.

Aimlessness, Loneliness, and Being Lost

The basic thesis and theme of much modern writing is, as all recognize, the loneliness, anxiety, and aimlessness of many men and women in our society. From *Rabbit Run* to *Couples* to *Small Changes,* the theme is the same. Sociologists from David Reisman in *The Lonely Crowd* to Peter Berger in *The Human Shape of Work,* and psychologists, theologians, and moralists have emphasized the cut-off-from-one-another nature of the modern person's life. Every new (or revised) philosophy, religion, and liberation movement has zeroed in on this failure of goal and lack of community as the mortal enemies of human good. Theologians agree, from Paul Tillich, who wrestled with anxiety to arrive at *The Courage to Be,* to Harvey Cox with his recommendation of playfulness in *The Feast of Fools* and of "people's religion" in *The Seduction of the Spirit.*

Loneliness is a problem, even a major one. Aimlessness, too, is frightening in its spread and hateful effects on our daily lives. I see this lack of aim and goal as increasing, not decreasing, particularly among college-age youth and, increasingly, among the middle classes, who had already made some sort of compromise with life. Drug and alcohol abuse (the latter surpassing the former), divorces, and runaway young people, the rise of more crimes against the person in both urban and suburban areas, all point to growing aimlessness. A vehicle without aim is bound to collide eventually with other unguided vehicles. Too many of us are truly accidents looking for a place to happen. Random violence of a planned or accidental sort is to be expected from people without motivation and goal. A visit to any campus will reveal the depth of apathy among the younger generation. The public's response to Watergate shows the apathy of large segments of the population.

But what is the real reason for this state of affairs? Social scientists are long on analysis and anecdotal documentation but short on practical solutions to the problems they isolate. Theologians and literary critics are long on moralistic tut-tutting but point, in vague and high-sounding ways, only to our need to return to the Lord or to recover the high culture our ancestors were supposed to have. I think returning to the Lord and recovering culture are both fine things, as is sociological analysis also, but all these pointing fingers miss the vital step of showing us the underlying cause of loneliness and meaninglessness.

That cause, once it is felt in the depths of the personality, can be turned into the answer to our question. The cause of our painful—or even feeling-less—isolation from one another and from constructive goals, is our loss of contact with our inner fantasy life. Cut off from the depths of ourselves, the real source of feelings and the wellspring of motivation, we can do no more than fake community and adherence to goals on the conscious, public level. Everything we say and do becomes purely other-directed, in terms of influence on our behavior and of the direction of our response. Without submergence in our own inner vision we become the "puppet man" of the popular song, living in "ticky-tacky" boxes, going through the motions of belonging. The man or woman who is participating in the creative flow of his or her inner fantasies and daily developing the plot of his or her personal story is able both to think and to feel. Such a person can belong, in the sense of membership in a group of other feeling persons, and not just belong as a possession of the state or tribe. We err in crying out to belong to something; the human relation is *membership, participation* in the pooled psychic lives of those we help to sustain and who help to sustain us. Life together is not giving and taking, it is *sharing.* He who is most inward is most adult in outward relationships.

St. Augustine long ago pointed out that before we can love our neighbor as we love ourselves we must love ourselves. Lack of proper self-love prevents us from ever really loving others. We, too, stand in the need of prayer and love, not just the other. Before we try either to sell ourselves to others or to give ourselves away, we need to become persons worth sharing with other persons. Membership in the sharing sense is the equivalent of love. The blind that seek to help the blind become hazards not only to blind people, but to the seeing also.

Literature and Life

Modern literature is like St. Paul's darkened glass, through which we see ourselves dimly, distortedly. This is meant to be no slur on literature, since most of us are dim and distorted figures of humanity and the society we have created bears the marks of its creators. Herman Hesse holds up the mirror, and it is not Alice's looking glass but a psychoanalytic prism as clear as that of Alfred Adler or Wilhelm Reich, showing us the schizophrenic character of our inner experience. We would be the cultured and quiet student, a problem to no one, and the wild wolf obliterating everyone who gets in our path, at one and the same time. Berne and Harris, as well as Freud and Jung, have shown us the same self-portrait. The hostility and repressed anger that reveal themselves in games and ploys and slips of the tongue are really there, whether a doctor or a novelist holds up the glass. Hesse's Steppenwolf is split; his inner life and outward activity are not in harmony. The wolf is the more tortured, measured by the lives of most of us, only because he is still in touch with the fantasies within him; he is more open to his instinctual feelings. Magister Ludi, the intellectual bureaucrat, the Harvard professor turned assistant president, is not as whole as the wolf. His every human feeling was systematically discarded for the good of the order, for the good of the future. He deliberately suppressed the past and ignored the present. All that was random or natural he disciplined into order. He was American to the core.

The personal fantasies we shape our lives by derive, in many ways, from the family fantasy, the basic philosophic worldview we absorbed with our childhood food and our earliest religious ideas. The stories we are telling to ourselves and to the world are more influenced by our culture and religion than many individualistic secularists would like to admit. Carl G. Jung spoke of the recurring symbols of our inner life, and this discussion tends to bear out the existence of images like the Indian, the border, and the sacred meal in our fantasy lives. Moreover, every one of us has the same inward temptations, weaknesses, desires, and needs. When we get ourselves together, in touch with our inner lives, we find that all of us live, work, play, write, and create out of the same materials of the mind, evil and good, that are as old as mankind.

4

Tell Me a Story

THE OUTER WORLD:
MANIFESTATION OF THE INNER WORLD

During the summers that my family shared the joys of
nature and community at Holden Village, a Christian
retreat center in the High Cascades of Washington State,[1]
one of the favorite activities of the children was the daily
"story-telling" in the old schoolhouse fitted up for arts and
crafts. Named for one of C. S. Lewis' creations, the school
boasted the sign "Narnia" and lived up to its claims.
People everywhere tell stories and listen to storytellers.
Americans and Canadians today still do this, though it is
our misfortune to listen more than tell—and to listen to an
electronic box instead of a human voice—most of the
time. If the medium is the message, or anything resembling
the message, then it is no wonder that we are producing a
schizoid and separated society.

Against the solitary and mainly silent viewing of the television I would seriously pit the pleasures of play and work together, of mutual storytelling, the kind of chaotic comfort I recorded in the following poem about our Holden Village experiences.

Snuggle

Young boys crowd around the phonograph;
The hard rock clashes with
               the contentment on their faces.
Broad-beamed babes and their shouldered gallants
huddle up to sauna rocks,
               the fever of the day cooling on and
under the pressure of the braising heat.
The mother rubs her nose against the infant's cheek.
The swimmers struggle through stones to creek.
The mustachioed man draws the ripened blonde
to him with an oblique glance.
The youngsters—in their own world—push and prance,
landing blows of love on side and back
               at every chance.
The old dog sleeps half in, half out the sun,
               nose snuggled up to tail which twitches on.
The grass grasps the shallow soil
Like lover's distracted fingers
enmeshed in faded hair

Life pulls close to warm and soft
               to wet and loud
in flesh or flood
To actualize in outward terms
The oneness throbbing in the blood.

In the rough and tumble of fellowship there may be little of the peace that the urbanites' jangled nerves cry out for, but there is a peace that satisfies, passing all our modern understanding. In talking with each other we can put a ceremonial song of the Pawnee Indians to the test:

> Let us see, is this real,
> Let us see, is this real,
> This life I am living?
> Ye Gods, who dwell everywhere,
> Let us see, is this real,
> This life I am living?

Life together in storytelling very often moves us to poetry, the true language of the inner life, as saints like Francis and Soldiers of Fortune like Lawrence of Arabia have demonstrated throughout history. And in poetry we may find the ability to have fellowship and share our stories in silence.

To begin to tell your story you need only begin to look within yourself more intently, while looking outside yourself more contentedly. As long as you look with competitiveness upon those around you, you will never have time to develop your inner story. Your heart is a window, but a window that clouds up when it is filled with envy and comparisons. Amazingly, our heart is also a lens through which we can pierce through the outer shells of our fellows when we have cleansed it of aggressiveness and desire. The inwardly looking person need not be solitary, a monk or a selfish person cut off from others. Rather, that one who is most actively contemplating himself in a spirit of good will towards others will vibrate in empathy to the heartbeats around him.

Poetry

> Not in the depth of thought alone,
> Nor in the sensory brush of flesh;

Neither in the voiceless fear
or temple throb of ecstasy,
But in, with, and through these all
The poet that you are now calls
Your story into existence.

Your story is the residue that remains when the mass of
your experience is strained through the holes worn in your
spirit by the shocks and cares of life. The ancient Greeks
had a myth to this effect, telling of a huge, hollow, golden
bull, which was filled with youths to be sacrificed. A fire
was built under this hollow statue, and as the heat rose
inside, the screaming of the prisoners escaped through
holes in the mouth of the bull. This suffering screaming,
transmuted by the metal of the statue, sounded like a
beautiful melody. Our inner story is very much like that.
Our failures, defeats, and sufferings can be transmuted by
spirit into beauty and satisfaction. Viktor Frankl, the
psychiatrist who survived the Nazi death camps, tells us
the same thing in *From Death Camp to Existentialism*.[2]
Nonetheless, we must beware of turning beauty into
banality, gold into lead. There are "stories" that reduce
this universal insight into shallow sentimentality. "The
Little Engine Who Could," who lumbered up the moun-
tainside puffing, "I think I can, I think I can," is a sound
enough story for little children, but it is slop when turned
into pseudo-philosophy in *Jonathan Livingston Seagull*.
  It is so easy to say words without meaning. When I
recommend telling a story, telling your story, I don't mean
to praise small talk. Like everyone else, I am profoundly
tired of the small talk of the street, party, office, classroom,
and back fence by the week's end. A Quaker silent
meeting often seems more desirable than a sermon at
times like that. Yet it is not story but words that have

turned me off. A sermon that cuts to the depths, a play that reveals the heart, a movie or even television show that shows and involves and doesn't just tell, refreshes me from my surfeit of words. Poetry, in particular, is a solace at such points. I do believe that poetry is the natural language of mankind and that our inner story is told in poetry.

Peter Farb has given us an excellent study of language in *Word Play, What Happens When People Talk.* Farb points out an obvious, but usually overlooked fact, that all people are creative in their use of language, so that, in our terms, everyone's story can be and is different. He remarks:

> Not every human being can play the violin, do calculus, jump high hurdles, or sail a canoe, no matter how excellent his teachers or how arduous his training—but every person constantly creates utterances never before spoken on earth. Incredible as it may seem at first thought, the sentence you just read possibly appeared in exactly this form for the first time in the history of the English language—and the same thing might be said about the sentence you are reading now. In fact, if conventional remarks—such as greetings, farewells, stock phrases like Thank you, proverbs, cliches, and so forth—are disregarded, in theory all of a person's speech consists of sentences never before uttered.[3]

Our originality and creativity as persons cannot be denied. I love every excursion into the world just because every visit reveals the outlandish ingenuity of people. I have seen people build houses of old beer cans, make a living from the trash heaps of armies and coax ruined motor cars into a second life. Yet our stories are marked by ugliness, selfishness, hatefulness, and pain. The cat who plays with a captured mouse is creative, too. I have thought, at length, about the dissonance of our individual and social stories.

We gain little ground in telling ourselves our stories if we pretend that the fatal flaw of sin is not there. I think one of our finest social critics, Philip Slater, has hit on the nature of man's disruptive, destructive career in the world in his book *Earthwalk*. Slater sees the crucial importance of recognizing our fantasy lives since he sees our activities in the world as the projection and materialization of our fantasies. Quoting Norman O. Brown, Slater observes,

The self . . . is maintained by constantly absorbing good parts . . . from the outside world and expelling bad parts from the inner world.[4]

Applying this insight to the problem of environmental pollution, Slater says:

Pollution is an inescapable part of humanity's relationship with the environment—our very identity rests upon psychic pollution, just as our physical integrity rests upon expelling organic wastes.[5]

Slater goes on to develop the thesis that mankind's problems are due to the ability of man to materialize fantasy. This is an important insight, a clear statement of the true source of pollution, war, social inequality—all the vices and devices that bedevil us at every turn. Out of the heart flow the issues of life.

The danger arises when a man's psychic excretions are given material form, when his projections appear as physical objects. We cannot ignore his fantasies of super potency when they are represented by overpowered automobiles that claim a thousand lives a week; his paranoid fears when they are expressed in bugging devices and security data banks; his hatreds when they appear in the form of a nuclear arsenal capable of eliminating vertebrate life on our planet.

Our psychic excretions, in other words, show an annoying tendency to become part of our real environment, so that we are forced to consume our own psychic wastes in physical form.[6]

Watergate might be said to have had its genesis in former President Nixon's belief that "Nobody is a friend of ours," and World War II its origin in the belief that the nations of Europe desired to deprive the German people of "living room" and the Japanese Empire of "raw materials." The story we tell ourselves long enough becomes the story that everyone else in the world has to finish. We inevitably bring the rest of mankind into the making of our movie.

I think we can structure our stories so that the effect they will have upon others will be for good, not evil, and that it is our life's task to do just that.

For a writer, every incident brings to mind a chain of associations from past experiences. I can never look at dented cans without recalling my one far-reaching experience with hunger and sharing, the campaign in North Korea, November–December, 1950. I remember that on our way up the valleys far from our sea-borne supplies we were short of rations. Three Marines shared one small can of rations together. It wasn't much, but the genuine sharing was very moving. Later, on the way out through those same valleys, I was without any food for several days. I was cold and tired, and like the Greeks in Xenophon's *Anabasis*, searched the ground of the road and the dirty snow for any little thing to eat. One day I saw a ration can. On picking it up I found a bit of lima beans and ham in the bottom of it. It was delicious.

Mankind's clearest lesson is, don't waste food, but its dearest lesson is share.

Kurt Vonnegut has written, "be careful what you pretend to be, for that's what you will become." This is the same insight as that of Philip Slater. The world around us is produced of materialized fantasies. Everyday the evidence supporting this contra-materialist truth mounts higher. Jan Morris (once the male author, James Morris) writes in *Conundrum*, the dramatic story of her sex change from man into woman:

I was for the time being a kind of non-human, a sprite or monster, as you wish; so when the world oppressed me I left it, and wandering through other fields of sensibility, . . . I insulated myself against misfortune. Harmless lying, I found, was itself a panacea. Either people believed me when I said I had a unicorn at home, or they thought me crazy, or they called me a liar, or they accepted the fancy for itself; and by offering them four distinct choices, the lie diverted their attention from mistier enigmas behind, and excused me too from specifics. After all, my life was one long protest against the separation of fact from fantasy: fantasy was fact, I reasoned, just as mind was body, or imagination truth.[7]

The reality that Morris conjured up for his/her fantasies ultimately included an operation that turned him into a female. This realization of a life-long dream seemingly has made Jan very happy.

Not all of us are made happy by the realization of fantasy, however. The people shot dead and wounded by the man in the Texas tower were part of his realized, materialized fantasy. Being part of someone else's movie is a chancy thing. The degradation that can be wrought when we project our fantasies onto others is graphically portrayed by Donald Bogle in *Toms, Coons, Mulattoes,*

Mammies and Blacks. Bogle shows us what Hollywood did to the image of the American Negro by projecting the ignorance and prejudice of whites against blacks upon the screen. The author shows us the stereotypes of the public's view of blacks as "the dying slave content that he has well served the massa." [8] From the self-demeaning comics to shuffling servants to sex objects, the camera materialized the de-humanizing fantasies of the (white) majority about blacks in society. I'm not at all sure that the super-masculine, aggressive-heroic film characters like "Superfly" are any more healthy projections of fantasy, but at least they are different.

Once we begin to see the world around us as the materialization of projected fantasies, we have a clue not only to the economic and sexual exploitation of our society, and to its architecture and politics, but also to the life scenarios of people we know. I had a friend who taught in a rural area of the Dakotas and hated it. He had always painted, and thought of himself as an artist. During his university days in Minneapolis he haunted the art museums but studied for a different career. Perhaps people told him there was no future in painting. In all events, in his inner fantasy life he was an artist. The reality of his work with pragmatic people galled him so much that he declared he must go into painting, or die. He did make the break, moved to California, and took a master's degree in painting. This was a great sacrifice on his part as well as by his family. My friend was very happy. I received a letter from him saying so just after he graduated, but in the same envelope was a note from his wife and a copy of his funeral service. His motorcycle was struck by a car the day he wrote me the letter. He "became" an artist and died. All those years longing to turn fantasy into fact, because it was fact, were suffered through to lead to that beginning-end on a California street. I like to think that he was happy. I just wish he had started telling his real story sooner.

A BAD STORY CAN BLIGHT MANY LIVES

My son, a colleague, and I were at a health club, running from steam room to sauna to pool. I lay down beside the whirlpool and began to pass the time of day with an elderly man. This gentleman knew I was a clergyman and wanted to tell me a story about his Methodist clergyman grandfather. It turned out that it was a story about the story that his grandfather imposed on three generations—to the harm of all.

The grandfather took the Bible literally, but oddly, when he read that man was conceived in sin and born in iniquity. He loved all his children except one son, my storyteller's father, for he felt that this child's birth resulted from a peculiarly lustful episode with his wife. Such an idea was bad enough, but he compounded it by telling the story to his son, and by refusing ever to have him baptized. Told that he was bad all through his childhood, the boy ran away from home just as soon as he was able. Later he married a Roman Catholic girl, which the bigoted minister took as confirmation of his judgment of the boy. Indeed, after my friend and his brothers and sisters came along, the grandfather managed to poison them also with the story of their father's "vile" birth. It took years for my friend to overcome this evil effect. I was frankly amazed at this story and felt that my life-long opposition to religious literalism and bigotry was affirmed as not only just, but mentally healthy too. This report underscores the evil that a wrong-headed personal story can have, setting the children's teeth on edge generations after the fathers have eaten sour grapes. Thank God that a wholesome story can have the very opposite effect!

Many of us today are beginning to recognize the inexorable march of time. We do not want to die without ever having played out that inner fantasy that troubles our routine days and soothes us on empty nights. We can respond to Henry David Thoreau's explanation for moving from town to Walden Pond. Thoreau painted the mood of the inner directed person (and yet outwardly oriented also) quite vividly, saying:

> I went to the woods because I wished to live deliberately, to front only the essential facts of life, and see if I could not learn what it had to teach, and not, when I came to die, discover I had not lived.[9]

Thoreau gave up what he saw as a life of urbanized luxury and protection in the interests of uncovering the human parts of himself, in order to develop a fuller consciousness of and participation in a deeper mode of human life.

Hundreds of people over the past few years have emulated Thoreau, and the lure of this "plain person" movement towards a simpler life[10] has influenced the recreational and eating habits of thousands more. Don Biggs has documented some of this social upheaval in *Breaking Out . . . Of a Job You Don't Like . . . And the Regimented Life.* Biggs reports having talked with more than one hundred and fifty corporate executives and former executives as well as psychologists and executive recruiters. He says:

> In certain key respects, the finding of our on-the-record interviews with men who've stepped out of the company

organization chart were similar to our off-the-record talks with executives who feel boxed in by their present positions in the corporate hierarchy. Increasingly, good men give up sizable paychecks and challenging jobs because: They feel they are slipping away from themselves, caught up in a corporate role that leaves less and less room in their lives for them to be "real." [11]

This is a major syndrome of what Slater calls the schizoid society. It is an indication to me that the role play exacted of men and women in our society prevents the development of those eccentricities and idiosyncrasies that make a person a real individual, a unique member of a group (not just an interchangeable part)—in short, that this role play keeps us from telling our inner story to ourselves and materializing it in the world around us. Slater opines, convincingly I think, that nature heals itself by periodically flushing its system, including the social system, by movements that begin at the unconscious level not by fads or five-year plans, but by the movement of life itself. Some of these healing processes are decentralization, deceleration, and depolarization.[12] The upsurge of inner fantasies into the personal actions and social movements which mark our present decade is surely a result of such processes, especially of depolarization. The women's lib movement, often seen as polarizing, is actually a wave of depolarization through the sensitizing and "consciousness expanding" of both men and women. As Slater says, "During periods of crisis the forms of specialization that we have learned to accept as the natural order of things must often be dissolved." [13]

To see the process of depolarization and sensitization from the inside, Jan Morris' book is a must-read exposé. The novels of Marge Piercy are other records from the struggle for depolarization that ought to be read. As Thomas Pynchon has said of Piercy, "Here is somebody with the guts to go into the deepest core of herself, her time, her history, . . . just out of a love for the truth and a need to tell it." [14]

One of Piercy's characters in *Small Changes*, Beth, lives in her daydreams:

She knew there was something shameful about living so much in daydream, not only because she was returning to a period she thought she had outgrown in meeting Jim, but because there was something second rate about an imaginary life. Her best thinking was going not into living but into making up lives. All the rest of that Sunday she forced herself to fight daydreaming. Yes, daydreaming was a drug. It kept her quiet, it made the time pass better than being stoned.

By refusing to let herself dream away that Sunday she remained conscious of it. Conscious of the housework and how weary she was of doing it while he sat and watched her, littering the floor she had just cleaned and then complaining if the litter remained. . . .

There had to be more than this! They were not really together. This could not be what they had wanted.[15]

Rosemary Haughton comes at the problem of freeing ourselves so as to deal with the fantasy realm, our deepest, most personal center, the real "me," in her study of fairy tales and the spiritual search, *Tales From Eternity*. Ms. Haughton tells us of the character or symbol of the fairy tale princess, who is a symbol of the genuine Christian's mode of being-in-the-world precisely because she is very sensitive to what is wrong in society. She writes:

The long history of the church is starred with martyrs who died, sometimes at the hands of other Christians, because they

were real princesses and could not rest content when they felt a
lump that no one else noticed under the mattresses of public
apathy. . . . Beginning with Stephen, the first martyr, who
refused to stop pointing out what was wrong with first-century
Judaism, many names occur. . . . Thomas More and John
Bunyan spring to mind, and, nearer our own time, Dietrich
Bonhoeffer and Franz Jagerstetter, Protestant and Catholic, who
both saw through the Nazi myth and died in consequence.[16]

I find it interesting that Thomas More and John Bunyan
both opposed the myths of their day by recourse to
fantasy. *Utopia* and *Pilgrim's Progress* are genuine projections of the inner fantasy worlds and the deepest religious
feelings of More and Bunyan. These were men who, like
Bonhoeffer, looked within and found the God of history at
work in their lives so clearly that they could not remain
silent when his name was taken in vain by the pseudo-
mythology of the day. Ms. Haughton speaks of such
people as spiritually mature. She calls our attention to
"great Christian women (who) have very often been the
predominantly 'energetic princess' type," such as Joan of
Arc, Teresa of Avila, Octavia Hill, and Gladys Aylward.[17]
Telling your story will be exciting, to be sure, but it may
also, as Ms. Haughton has pointed out, be painful. The
cartoon film mentioned earlier, "The Man Who Had to
Sing," makes the toughness of the life experience of the
inner directed person profoundly clear. Bonhoeffer, the
Christian "princess" of World War II, said:

Every day brings to the Christian many hours in which he will
be alone in an unchristian environment. These are the times of
testing. This is the test of true meditation and true Christian
community. . . .
Furthermore, this is the place where we find out whether the
Christian's meditation has led him into the unreal, from which

he awakens in terror when he returns to the workaday world, or whether it has led him into a real contact with God, from which he emerges strengthened and purified. Has it transported him for a moment into a spiritual ecstasy that vanishes when everyday life returns, or has it lodged the Word of God so securely and deeply in his heart that it holds and fortifies him, impelling him to active love, to obedience, to good work? Only the day can decide.[18]

Bonhoeffer poses here the question that all religious people must direct to their worship and prayer life. Do I engage in unreality when I sing, read scripture, and pray—together or alone? Or do I reach the very depths of my personal story, down to the floor, the source, the ground of my very being, God? And if I do reach God, do I answer his call in my life? For the "Christian princess," for the person striving to be "real," there can be only one answer. As Bonhoeffer decided, we must decide: "If a drunken driver is at the wheel, it is not just the minister's job to comfort the relations of those he has killed, but if possible to seize the steering wheel." [19] It is in this movement from the inward to the outward, in the materialization of our fantasies into actions, that most of our denial of Christian faith, and of inner authenticity as persons takes place.

SOAP OPERAS AND NEGLECTED FANTASIES

The fairy tale is hardly a group of pleasing stories designed to keep children happy. A moment's reflection will show you the non-childish nature of most genuine fairy tales. The old stories are full of bloodshed, horror, and thinly disguised sexuality. Fairy tales are the deposits of the group consciousness of our European ancestors, a code-language for the fantasies of man's sufferings in the world and of the best ways to overcome them. Fairy tales are highly concentrated doses of folk wisdom designed to strengthen the psyches of the young and the not-so-young, when they need such fortification. Today fairy tales have been supplemented almost to the point of being replaced by the Walt Disney-like modern fantasy and adventure tale for children, and the soap opera, horse opera, and detective tale for all ages. The tube and the screen beam these homogenized fantasies at us night and day, and in inadequately matured people, they replace the personal fantasy life with their stereotyped schemes for coping with the world. "Popular Culture," a term recently coined by academic types,[20] deals with the structure and content of these "plays."

As we noted in discussing Donald Bogle's study of the Negro in Hollywood films, the mass entertainment media (radio and television "soaps," adventure series, and movies) play up to the projected fantasies (including prejudices) of the majority public. The criteria of community interpretation, of what is expected of people of various races, nationalities, classes, and sexes forms the imagery pattern of such stories. The old bandit laughed at Gary Cooper in *For Whom the Bell Tolls* when Gary said he was a college professor. "A professor," the scoundrel cried. "He has no beard. A professor has a beard!" We may have progressed a bit beyond that shallow type of identification, but not much. The recent Supreme Court rulings on pornography, making local community standards the criteria of obscenity, really push the mass media into even more shallow symbols of personality and life.

Harold Mendelson, writing in *Mass Entertainment* says of popular fiction:

For the middle and upper middle classes, mass entertainment that is dominated by middle class symbolism can be seen as serving a legitimizing function in the sense that it acts to reinforce the general merits of middle class life and to reassure members of the middle classes of the worth of the lives they are now leading.[21]

There isn't much challenge to become a more "real" person in entertainment like that. However, Stephen C. Holder has observed that "popular taste can be a demanding mistress; it vacillates wildly and rapidly in some areas at the same time it remains relatively constant in others." [22] The wild swings of popular culture we call "fads" come and go, and trouble be to him or her who invests too much time, energy, or money in a fad! We sometimes hear about businessmen with warehouses full of hula-hoops and Davy Crockett caps that wouldn't sell when the fads changed.

The soap operas and the horse operas, for all their stereotyping of personalities, seem responsive to popular cultural changes. Perhaps they can do this because of their constant exposure to a mass public and the constant feedback of fan letters to their producers. Another possibility is that the symbols of sex and violence that they deal with are so basic to American culture that they are relatively immortal. The cap guns which children today play with, modeled on the weapons carried by cowboy heroes and detectives, are not very different from the ones I played with as a boy. I daresay sex hasn't changed much except for the frankness with which we discuss it publicly.

I see the daytime soap operas on television and the Westerns and police stories as aiming at different fantasy dimensions in the public mind. With Zane Grey, the Western series sees nature as a purifying force, wiping away the corruption of urbanization, taking man back to the struggle of the fittest to survive. The police story, by and large, pits the natural "wholesomeness" of the policeman against the same urbanized corruption, the hero wiping corruption away with his pistol, or putting it out of sight behind bars. On the other hand, the "soaps" aim at exploring the corruption of the human heart, trying to show that there is adultery in all of us, even the most respected members of society. The large numbers of medical doctors who are shown to be sexually involved with nurses and their patients are a sign of this hidden agenda.

What these popular myths and fantasies do is to confirm for the viewer the feeling that "I'm not so bad; other, more respectable people do what I do—or want to do." The violent aspect tends to concretize evil and so categorize it out of our lives. Evil people aren't the everyday people who take advantage of one another sexually but are the members of organized gangs, bank robbers, and other easily identified persons. There isn't much room for personal reflection and growth in such fantasies.

Sam Keen and Anne Valley Fox take a different tack in *Telling Your Story.* Keen and Fox encourage us to use our fantasy-power, to tell our story and not to excuse ourselves from grappling with the hard questions of life. In words very similar to Slater's warnings about the schizoid society, they say:

Imagination is an incorrigible child forever at play with frivolities when reason is doing serious work. Daydreams wander in and out of consciousness, interrupting concentrated thought. As rationality gains exclusive control over our lives we drive out our daydreams. They are flights from reality into fancy, trips taken at the expense of the boss, the job, the problem that has to be solved. All true . . . they are disturbers of the peace, but we ignore them at our own peril. Without them the psyche shrivels. . . .

Desires range from split-second spasms to lifelong intentions. Some desires lead to action; others linger or wear themselves out in fantasy. Imagine a scale of desire. The weakest desires are fleeting, wishes, such as: "I wish I could fly, . . ." Wants are one degree stronger than wishes: "I really want to have a baby, . . ." Willing and deciding are manifestations of even stronger desires. . . . Action is the final stage in the realization of desire. . . .

Fantasy can be an economical way of trying on alternative ways of feeling, acting, and being. . . .

Paradoxically, when we stay in touch with our most outrageous fantasies our path toward realistic goals is most direct. When we allow the child within us free play it is easier to enjoy our self-chosen responsibilities.[23]

BREAKING THROUGH

I think that I have quoted enough authorities and practitioners of the arts of personal fantasy to demonstrate that I am not recommending some schizophrenic self-delusion. Actually, fantasy and the cultivation of it are the sanest activities we can engage in. But the point to be underscored is that such an exercise of fantasy is to lead us on to deeper, better realized actions and relationships in the social and natural worlds around us. It is not to separate us from nature and mankind more than we are already separated. Fantasy, pursued with an active imagination, should lead us to empathy with others. As Marcus Aurelius wrote long ago, "As you are a component part of a social system, so let every act of yours be a component part of social life." [24]

In short, "I, too, am a man (a person) and nothing that has to do with mankind is foreign to me." Our story is very similar to the stories of others, and as I want to conclude my story in happiness and full realization of every healthful desire, so, too, I rejoice in every completed story that is told. It does take imagination to feel empathy— imagination and a feeling for the wholeness of life in the world.

Richard Adams shows this empathy, this feeling for the interconnectedness of life in his justly popular novel, *Watership Down*.[25] Adams paints a picture of the human social world using rabbits as characters. Fiver, an intuitive, prophetic little rabbit looks at the hill they live on, one evening, and in his mind's eye, he sees it covered with blood. His brother, Hazel, thinks this is only the glare of the setting sun, but Fiver knows better. He immediately calls upon the rabbits of the warren to flee away. Most do not listen, but some follow on to new adventures. The soundness of Fiver's vision is confirmed by the legend on a sign posted in the midst of the rabbit's area. The sign announces the coming construction of a new housing project. That will be the end of the world that the rabbits have always known.

Another voyager of the imagination is Robert Farrar Capon, Episcopal priest and seminary professor. Father Capon has given us a fresh insight into the Christian religion with his fanciful book, *Hunting the Divine Fox: Images and Mystery in Christian Faith*. I've had a lot of fun with seminary classes using Capon's fantastic imagery of the human situation *vis-à-vis* God. He describes the person who lusts after knowledge of the Divine as an oyster living in the mud of a tidal pool. In attempting to make logical sense of what the realm of the spirit must be like, our "thinking oyster" comes to syllogisms like:

Starfish move; ballerinas move.
Starfish are deadly to oysters.
Are ballerinas deadly to oysters? [26]

How the oyster gets to ideas like this is the gist of
Capon's insight into the pomposity of human reasoning.
Needless to say, Capon ought to be read by everyone who
presumes to talk about (for or against) God.

Fantasy is alive and well in theology, as we can see, as
well as in recent literary fiction. Besides the beautiful and
moving story of the rabbit seekers in *Watership Down*,
there is Geoffrey Ashe's *The Finger and the Moon* and Joan
Phipson's *The Way Home*. Just as *Watership Down* introduces us to a world where we are identified with a group of
rabbits, and we are taken, in fantasy, for a tour of their
world, so *The Finger and the Moon* introduces us to a
human sub-world where genuine magic is practiced. Joan
Phipson's adventure into fantasy takes us through a series
of accidents with three young people who suddenly find
themselves outside the usual space-time matrix of our
world. They find themselves journeying to strange places
and into prehistoric times. Indeed, Ms. Phipson introduces
us to a time-place where a spirit, an unknown presence
hovers over the youth, helping them in uncanny ways that
two of the young folk find natural and only one thinks
disturbing.

In fantasy mankind runs through myriad forms of the
future in alternative guises. It is the real essence of
the writer's work to give us all an opportunity to try on the
many lives that the rich fantasy life of the creative person
can project upon the structures of the present.

Our writers are writing. Perhaps we ought to be reading
more.

In imagination and fantasy we can reach out and live

alternative lives. We can come to walk in the sandals (or with the paws) of other creatures, if only for a few moments. Such brief alternative lives make us fuller, more satisfied, and more tolerant human beings. Empathy, sympathy, friendship, love, all rest on this ability to project one's self into the life situation of another. If we do not love, it may well be because we lack the imagination for it. Richard Adams, Sam Keen, and many other contemporary sensitive writers are offering us assistance toward the development of our imaginations.

Just think of it: In imagination, through fantasy, you can live many lives while developing the inner story that is your most profound life. Nothing need be strange to you, not science, not war, not art, not travel, not your neighbor, not even death.

5

Making a Good End

BEYOND THE EASTER BUNNY

My youngest son walked into my study the Thursday before Easter and announced, "Now I believe in the Easter Bunny." When I asked why, he replied that he had found a rabbit in the woods that was so gentle he let himself be picked up. Paul reported that he dug the bunny a hole and took him some carrots.

I hadn't believed in the Easter Bunny myself for some time and most of the wild rabbits I've seen run away when you approach them. I became concerned that my son had been handling a sick animal, so we went to see Paul's bunny.

We found the rabbit a few feet from the new hole Paul had dug. Our bunny was lying in some water and didn't flee when we approached. Upon examination I found that a dog or a car had injured the poor creature. We put it in a warm place, with food, and left it to the mercy of nature. There was nothing I could really do to help that bunny, but I couldn't kill it.

Paul and his friends already have spoken the hidden words: Maybe bunny will die. I suspect that he will. From skepticism to fantasy to reality is a long but rapidly traversed road. We travel that route every time we fall in love, buy in on a fad, or support a political candidate. We aren't nine years old when we do those things, however, and they usually don't involve coming face to face with death. Paul has just moved a long way toward maturity.

What concerns me is that I think I do believe in the Easter Bunny now, too. I don't want this experience to cause Paul to repress the fantasy life that is welling up inside him because of his chance encounter with a little brown rabbit who didn't run away. I think bunny has something to say to us about Easter and reality that makes fantasy more basic to our lives than ever before—but mature fantasy, not Walt Disney-like, simpering fantasy.

Bunny showed us all how to face life and death with gentleness. That's a hard lesson and I don't pretend to have learned it. When your muscles and bones will work well enough for fight or flight, you rarely stop to consider gentleness. Old age, sickness, injury, and death sometimes come slowly enough to teach us, as they taught the young Gautama, who became the Buddha, how to become wise.

Injury, sickness, and death are no strangers to me, but I have hardly yet become wise. No matter that I was thirty-two years old when Paul was born, he, like the child Jesus held up before his disciples, has raced past me and most of the rest of us toward the coming Kingdom. Daily visits to the sick in hospital and the crippled shut-ins at home, and endless months in combat, where friend and foe literally fell on every side, have not penetrated my shell to become part of my inner life story, as one encounter with a rabbit did for Paul.

God knows I have had my chances—most of us have. If we would only stop thinking so clearly and feel more deeply, we might also be able to say, "Now, I believe."

Perhaps I am the way I am because, like most of my generation, I moved from Walt Disney's artificial fantasies to skepticism, and never made it all the way to maturity.

At age seventeen I was full of the fantasy of the heroism of war. As scared as I was within, I never let it show when the live ammunition and hand grenades were handed out on board the troopship that carried us to Inchon, Korea in September, 1950. It seemed like a John Wayne movie; one boy even sharpened his kabar knife like Jim Bowie and stuck it between his leggings and his trousers (Marines didn't wear boots in 1950). We went ashore and into battle as if we were attending the Saturday matinee. After a day, Jim Bowie was dead. During the first night I had my chance with the wild rabbit. The man in the fighting hole with me was hit and bled all over me in dying. The glory of war and the fun of it ended for me right there. Unfortunately, I only contracted the service-connected disease of skepticism. It took a long time to grow up.

Everybody should have an Easter Bunny. There is no Easter without death first, and no really healthy inner fantasy life that doesn't take account of the world, the flesh, and the final encounter of all, death.

The personal life story has not only been our life-long guide, comfort, and entertainment; *it has been our life.* And making a good end for our story is the way the fully realized person completes his life. Our personal life story is not complete without the episode of our death. Words like these, I know, are not popular in view of our culture-wide denial of death. I wish to move beyond this cultural denial to a statement in agreement with Aristotle. Strange to say, this man dead over 2300 years is more in touch with the needs of our present and future than many of our living teachers. Aristotle in life was not noted for his physical courage. Upon the death of Alexander, when the city of Athens rose in revolt, threatening Aristotle because he had been Alexander's teacher, Aristotle fled to the country, to his mother's farm. Aristotle declared that he would not give the Athenians the chance to sin twice against philosophy. Nevertheless, he died soon after of stomach trouble, having attained the age of sixty-three years and ,more wisdom than all but a handful of men and women in history.

Part of that wisdom was a philosophical vision of life as growth, maturation, and decay. All things, Aristotle said, men and women included, aim towards their final end, the summing up when all potential has been actualized, the *telos*, death. This *entelechos* or "inner aim" (or end) was physical before it was biological and formed the basis for a psychological process, in purpose and growth, in mankind. In some persons this psychological process, I would suggest, rises to the conscious level of personal literature, to the working out of an inner story. I think Aristotle knew this, for he observed, "Count no man happy until you see him die."

LIFE REDUCED TO NUMBERS

Developing an awareness of our inner fantasies is not only a necessity for mental health, but for the preservation of some measure of personal freedom in our society. All the social forces push us towards conformity and feature-lessness. In a time when our every aspect and activity has been licensed, filed, and given a number, we all need to shout out our own version of ourselves loudly and clearly.

Think of the tyranny of numbers we all suffer under today. The most basic of our numbers is our Social Security number. For a long time, that was all the use that number had—to keep our Social Security retirement account. Then, in the past few years, the Social Security number began to be used to designate all manner of things—tying multitudes of our activities together under one computer number.

In my own case, my Social Security number also serves as:

My state driver's license number;
My military service number;
My account number for the Internal Revenue Service,
The State Internal Revenue Service, and
The city and township revenue system;
My employee number at the state university where I teach;
My faculty identification card number;
My identification number at the Savings and Loan Association where I have my mortgage and my savings accounts;
My account number with my broker, my file with the county hospital, and my hospitalization and medical care insurance cards.

If I wish to contact any branch of government, federal, state, or local, my Social Security number is needed. Indeed, even my business affairs are bound up with it, for I cannot receive royalties from the sale of my books without furnishing the publisher's business office with this ubiquitous number.

My memory, like that of many professors, is faulty.

Goodness help me if I ever forget my Social Security number! Someplace, sometime, if anyone cares to do so, a computer could be programmed to print out a record of everything of consequence that I have ever done simply by punching in those innocent-looking numbers.

I once joked about all the different numbers I had—wondering if I had lost my "essence" to these many digits. I had (or once had) besides the Social Security number, an Army serial number, a Marine Corps service number, a Veterans' Administration "C" number, a student number, a rank number in my graduating class, several auto license numbers, a phone number, a street number and a postal zip code number, a loan number, a Blue Cross number, a license number to operate a short-wave radio, a Civil Air Patrol officer's number, a Red Cross life-saving card number, a boat license number, a fishing license number, a trailer license number, a Selective Service number, and even a number on the box of offering envelopes from my church.

Indeed, my very blood was typed into a code—A positive. I suppose that it was inevitable that all (or almost all) of these numbers would be distilled into the number of all numbers—to follow us from the cradle to the grave—the Social Security number. Inevitable, but frightening nonetheless. Somehow we sense that the only actually immortal thing about us is our "number."

DEFERRING DEATH

The gossip of popular mythology is full of references to people who deferred death. We read about the soldier who makes it back to his own lines only to collapse and die. We hear of the mother or wife who hangs on to life until a son or husband comes home, then dies. Recently, a sociologist sought to measure the truth of these stories. David Phillips, assistant professor of sociology at the State University of New York's Stony Brook campus, compared birth dates with death dates for 348 famous Americans. He reasoned that famous people would look forward to their birthdays, so if there were significantly fewer deaths just before birthdays and more after birthdays, this might show that we can defer death if the motivation is strong. The statistics he gathered supported popular mythology. Fewer famous people died in any given month than we might expect.

Not only famous people, but average people seem capable of this postponement of dying day. For example, people may "stick around" to see important events. There are fewer deaths than expected in New York City before Yom Kippur, the Jewish Day of Atonement. There are fewer deaths in the United States just before Presidential elections.[1] Death may not be a completely involuntary experience. Our attitude toward ourselves and to the mark we have made in the world, and our assessment of the story we have told ourselves, may be an important factor in when and how we die.

Our common fear of and consequent denial of death in America is based on the poor job most of us do in telling ourselves our inner story. Although we may have allowed our lives to be reduced to numbers, the elements of a good story are present in every one of us. Aristotle suggested that everything within a living being, from an acorn to a man, is present from the beginning of that being's existence. That living being fulfills its purpose, and in the case of man, is fulfilled, when it unfolds all its potentialities and makes actual that which was only promised in the beginning. What Aristotle discussed physically, nutritionally, and biologically, I want to extend to the realm of psyche and spirit. Without telling ourselves the full and complete story we start out with in life, we do not fulfill our potentialities no matter what kinds and quantities of things we do and acquire.

Aristotle felt that a long life, full of learning, earning, children, and accomplishments, was the fulfillment man aimed towards. Once this way was attained, a man could die happy. Only the person himself could tell if he had fulfilled his potential. Knowing this, Aristotle reserved judgment on a person's happiness until after the full story was played out. If one did show this sign of a good end, Aristotle would say that that person had reached the chief end of man, happiness. His soul was complete, his story told. On this basis Aristotle denied the immortality of the soul, contradicting Plato, for there was nothing else to be achieved. Arguing in the other direction, Aristotle also taught that the death of the young was the greatest tragedy.

Whatever is the case for man twenty-three centuries ago or today, it is clear to me that no one wants to die before he has finished telling his personal story to himself. In the case of many of us, telling this story, developing our fantasies means working out our personal story in our lives—giving concrete actuality to our inner hopes and dreams. No person wants to die without ending his or her inner story. We do not want to die with unlived life left in us, but more, we do not want to die before the denouement, the final revelation of the meaning of it all, is experienced within. The ending of our story comes not when we run out of words, or consciously mark it "the end"; not even when we tie up all the loose ends of our affairs and interests, but in an ecstatic experience of self-transcendence. Death is overcome, accepted as part of one's life; one has put death behind him after such a concluding experience. Everything after that, whether sooner or later, is but a physical stoppage, a letting go. Death is represented in iconography, then, as we see it so often in experience, wearing a smile.

What frightens us about death and dying, even when (or especially when) we are not conscious of it, is our failure to reach this manifestation of meaning, the summing up and ending of our innermost fantasies, the last chapter of our personal story. It is not physical, mental, or even spiritual death that chills and repels our thought; meaninglessness is the reality in our horror of the shades. The meaninglessness so often spoken about in the past forty years is not some philosopher's nightmare, but the result of our common experiences of horror over lives that have no point.

In the absence of completing our personal story, missing the ecstatic moment of transcendence, we manufacture fears about death. Socrates recognized that long ago. Plato, writing of Socrates' last days in *The Apology*, has Socrates say:

Hitherto the divine faculty of which the internal oracle is the source has constantly been in the habit of opposing me even about trifles . . . and now as you see there has come upon me that which may be thought, and is generally believed to be, the last and worst evil. But the oracle made no sign of opposition . . . in nothing I either said or did touching the matter at hand [his capital case trial] has the oracle opposed me. What do I take to be the explanation of this silence? I will tell you. It is the intimation that what has happened to me is a good, and that those of us who think that death is an evil are in error. For the customary sign would surely have opposed me had I been going to evil and not to good.[2]

In another place, Socrates also remarked:

For the fear of death is indeed the pretense of wisdom, and not real wisdom, being a pretense of knowing the unknown; and no one knows whether death, which men in their fear apprehend to be the greatest evil, may not be the greatest good.[3]

Socrates went on to finish his course, to complete his story. Despite the blandishment of friends who did not want to see him die, Socrates refused to change his story at the end. He drank the poison cup prescribed by his death sentence.

He was beginning to grow cold about the groin, when he uncovered his face, for he had covered himself up and said—they were his last words—he said: "Crito, I owe a cock to Asclepius; will you remember to pay the debt?"
"The debt shall be paid," said Crito, "is there anything else?" There was no answer to this question, but in a minute or two a movement was heard, and the attendants uncovered him; his eyes were set, and Crito closed his eyes and mouth.
Such was the end . . . of our friend . . . of all the men of his time whom I have known, . . . the wisest and justest and best.[4]

Socrates' friends were sad. They did not want to see him go. The old soldier was not alarmed; he had seen many die at the battles of Potidaea, Amphipolis, and Delium in the Peloponnesian War. Knowing the effect of death on the body, he covered himself up, yet it was the living Crito who wept, not the dying Socrates.

What causes us to mourn about the death of others is the same primordial apprehension that makes us fear our own deaths, the feeling of loss, especially loss of that which is yet incomplete. Something is cut off from us, a part of our inner story dies when a friend or loved one meets death. Our story may also come to an aborted end—some widows or parents never really recover from a death in the family. The major part of one's inner personal story is either cut off completely or harshly pruned—modified beyond recognition. We have all seen such people, living their lives still within the invisible orbit of the dead one's routine: sons who never marry, keeping the old home, watching over the relics of that one whose story is ended. How much of this "caretaker" behavior in sons, daughters, and surviving spouses is to be explained as an overly dependent love and how much as a kind of magical behavior growing out of one's fear of his own death, psychiatrists would have to decide in each individual case. It is clear that the death of another, particularly one close to us, makes us think uncomfortably of our own death, forcing us to recognize how far we are from concluding our own personal story.

We do not want our lives to be, in Shakespeare's words, "a tale told by an idiot, full of sound and fury, signifying nothing." [5]

And we sense that this meaninglessness, this lack of significance comes to most of us from incompleteness, because all the potentialities are not yet realized although all the chapters have been finished and the climax reached and passed.

Shakespeare, too, recognized that life is a story—or, for him, a play: "Life's but a walking shadow, a poor player that struts and frets his hour upon the stage and then is heard no more." [6] Such an insight is hard to take if you consider yourself a nobody, but surely not if you know yourself to be a Shakespeare. Long after one's voice is stilled, the sounds of the words one wrote, the pulse of the emotions one evokes with syllables and verse goes on. It is the monuments of Ozymandias that decay, not the insights of the human spirit cast in words.

As Shakespeare saw life as a play, John Keats saw it as poetry, saying:

> When I have fears that I may cease to be
> Before my pen has glean'd my teeming brain,
> Before high-piled books, in charact'ry,
> Hold like rich garners the full ripen'd grain
> . . . then on the shore of the wide world
> I stand alone, and think
> Till love and fame to nothingness do sink.[7]

All people, not just poets and playwrights, share this sentiment; we want to become whole, to have meaning. It is important to us that the universe be changed, be added to, because we have lived. The vast reservoir of poetry (good and bad) that wells up from all kinds of people is the sign and signal of this quest for meaning.

Aristotle definitely shared Plato's (originally Socrates') belief that mankind quests for meaning, no matter how very differently the two evaluated man and life. Aristotle saw life as full and complete—at least potentially so—in this life, in this world. Plato saw the element of transcendence—and consequently saw God—as of more importance to life. Therefore everything in Plato is religious, revolving around the immortality of the soul and the sense of responsibility one feels to God.

For Plato, Socrates showed his happiness and his full self-realization in this life coupled with an expectation of a fuller realization in the spiritual world, beyond death. Yet his happiness depended upon his having honestly, fully told his inner story. Socrates could say, "I have not been disobedient to the inner voice."

Aristotle, too, recognized that the last chapter was all important, for only at the end could all the strands of one's life be drawn together and the full mystery of who one was be revealed—to oneself and to others.

T. S. Matthews, in *Great Tom*, makes an observation about T. S. Eliot and poets in general that says something about man's need to get his story out:

A poet, like the spider, spins his poem out of his own vitals. But a spider doesn't mass-produce its web. Why should a poet publish his poetry? Why should he want to? Shouldn't the relief of having concocted the poem suffice him? Obviously it does not. He wants others, as many others as possible, to see and share his expressed feeling and presumably applaud what he has done.[8]

The fact that people leave wills, notes, and in the case of writers, literary estates tells us that people do write with an eye on death. Stewart Alsop, the famous *Newsweek* columnist, consciously wrote with both eyes on death in *Stay of Execution*, an account of his terrible leukemia. Alsop opined:

Death is, after all, the only universal experience except birth, and although a sensible person hopes to put it off as long as possible, it is, even in anticipation, an interesting experience.[9]

But death is a whale of a lot more interesting if you have led an interesting life like Alsop. He had gotten to know "Uncle Thanatos," as he calls death, very well on parachute jumps into Occupied France during World War II. Like many people who have experienced war and hardship in the course of their careers, Alsop may have been "a little in love with death" all along.

Ernest Becker, also a terminally ill cancer patient, but a

trained and astute student of human nature in addition, speaks of the heroics of everyday life. Under the masks we wear, the masks of our personalities, competencies, and status, there is the fear of death—and the fear of the world, of life in general. Becker, interviewed in *Psychology Today* by Sam Keen, remarks that his life's work is an attempt to merge science and the religious perspective. He feels that because men do fear life and death, human evil arises out of people's attempts to deny this finitude, this mortality and affirm their significance.[10]

Becker recommends heroism to his fellowmen as a way of living humanely without creating unnecessary evil. By heroism he means: "To leave behind something that heightens life and testifies to the worthwhileness of existence." [11] But he also means:

that heroism involves seeing life in a religious perspective. . . . I don't think one can be a hero in any really elevating sense without some transcendental referent, like being a hero for God, or for the creative powers of the universe. The most exalted type of heroism involves feeling that one has lived to some purpose that transcends one. This is why religion gives the individual the validation that nothing else gives him.[12]

Orson Welles' great motion picture, *Citizen Kane*, illustrates the reluctance to die that is typical even of the person who is hugely successful in financial and social terms. It is not enough that the dying publisher has amassed power of great proportions and the wealth needed to live as fully as he pleases, he is troubled by the incompleteness of his inward fantasy life. Welles' artistry at movie direction takes us through the central character's life from dreaming innocence to a life of ruthless pursuit of power to the dreamless night of death, but it is a life undergirded by a broken, incomplete fantasy. All that quest and achievement was in pursuit of a forgotten personal fantasy, an imaginative childhood period of play with a sled.

T. S. Matthews remarks about the difference between the assessment that one person makes of his life, and the assessment that a close friend would make of that same life. Matthews observes:

And no matter how empathetic with Eliot the chosen biographer may be, his point of view as a biographer will differ, in Richard Ellmann's phrase, "from that mixture of self-recrimination and self-justification which the great writer, like lesser men and women has made the subject of his lifelong conversation with himself." [13]

But most of all no person can really get inside the mind of another person, no matter how close one might be to someone else. We can never know the depth of their joy, or the corrosion of their loneliness.

LONELINESS AND DEATH

Mark Twain once put into electric prose the basic fear of loneliness and death experienced by many troubled people in *The Mysterious Stranger*.[14] Numbers of children especially have a fear of being left alone, abandoned. A graduate student of mine once confessed in a public speech that as a child he had nightmares in which he came home from school and found the house empty and the neighborhood deserted. Abandonment is a very real fear, undermining the self-image and social adjustment of many. Ultimately, the fact of death affects this dread of loneliness. Never having experienced full human community during life, the expiring mind can only project ultimate forlornness upon the cosmos.

Mark Twain's sharp little story is not as well known as it should be. Twain writes of a young boy, stricken by fever, who is bedfast and must keep himself amused. Echoing Robert Louis Stevenson's "When I was sick and lay abed, I had two pillows at my head," Twain shows us the boy's lead soldier wars upon the bedspread. Suddenly the devil appears to the feverish boy. For Dostoyevsky, in the same century, the devil appeared as a well-bred gentleman down on his luck. *The Brothers Karamazov* shows us a Satan who has become a rationalist, a liberal, and a progressive well-wisher of mankind. Such was Satan to the upper-class Russian, but not to the Missouri agnostic. For Twain the devil is still the great tempter, the seducer away from faith. For all his intellectual horseplay and scoffing, the middle-American Homer had a Fundamentalist's view of Satan.

The devil leads the boy to solipsism; Twain's plot is as simple, and as demonic, as that. Solipsism is that extreme philosophical position that holds that nothing whatsoever exists in the universe but the thinking subject itself. Gradually, the boy is brought to doubt the existence of his aunt, his friends, his town, the state, the nation, the world—and, finally, God. Turning in his dream to the devil, the poor creature exclaims: "But I still have you!" The devil then replies, "No, you don't," and disappears.

The prospect of being utterly alone is good only for the ego too much bruised by the crowded conditions of urban life. To be totally alone is as good a definition of hell as we are ever likely to achieve.

APPOINTMENTS IN SAMARRA, SEOUL,
AND EVERYWHERE

Death comes when it wills and where it finds you. W. Somerset Maugham made this clear in his legend about Samarra, for the central character flees from Samarra to escape a prediction that death would meet him there. However, death meets him in the market place of another town, to their mutual surprise. As death grabs the man, he says, "I thought we had an appointment in Samarra." [15] Death often surprises us, in sober truth. Try as we may to avoid it, it comes.

A sergeant in my outfit during the capture of Seoul had everyone stay down in their fighting holes during a long night when the enemy was attempting to infiltrate our lines and escape the debacle of the North Korean Army. "Don't show yourselves, keep down," he instructed his young Marines. "Shoot anything that moves." Then, during the night, for some unknown reason, he got out of his hole and was shot.

Returning to my parish from a long trip, I received a phone call to come to a certain home because of a death during the night. I knew the head of the house was ninety-three years old and drew my own conclusions. Then the caller said, "It's the daughter." You can never be sure.

And sometime death surprises us by *not* coming, or by coming in an unexpected way. Newspaper files are full of stories about returned servicemen who survived years of brutal combat only to be killed in auto accidents their first weekend home. Life is paradoxical and so is death. I met a young soldier aboard a hospital ship who was sheathed in a body cast. He had a terrible chest wound and a shattered arm but retained a lively sense of humor. "I'll bet that leg hurts," he said to me. "Not as bad as that does," I replied, pointing to his cast. "It doesn't hurt as much as the plug of tobacco I swallowed the other day," he replied. "And this isn't as bad as the white gas I drank by mistake the other night," I told him.

Life and death rarely make logical sense. A shell falls and a dozen men are hurled to the ground. Ten get up relatively unhurt while two are dead. At the Wonson landing, Yellow Beach was cleared of mines by frogmen offshore and swept clean to the high water mark by Marine engineers. Once landed in their amphibious tanks, Marines began unloading equipment and ammunition. Three of them grew tired, sat down on a piece of timber, and literally disappeared in the explosion of one mine everyone had missed. You hold on to life by your fingernails until the very nails fall off, but you eventually lose your grip. It's best to have your story straight—and moving towards completion—all the time.

As pastors we often see what we might take as unfairness if we think life ought to follow a script. Immanuel Kant tried to understand life, and couldn't do it without positing God, who, he said, will have the last word. That's probably correct, yet it is our script, our inner life story that ought to concern us. Reinhold Niebuhr was right in saying we need to pray for the courage to change what we can change and the serenity to accept what we cannot change. Pastors and other concerned persons see the young mother dying of cancer, try to counsel the confused and grieving husband, and well up inside when they talk to the uncomprehending children. Incomprehensibility is the general rule when a young father kills himself, and his family can think of no adequate reason— at least not one they or you can understand. Why does someone you shared a picnic with on one weekend blow his brains out before the next weekend? We can only say we don't know. What the other person's story really is may be too well hidden from us.

We sit by bed after bed containing suffering people. Visions rise in our minds of the poor old lady wasting away with tuberculosis, of the middle-aged farmer who confesses his faith, receives communion, and then breaks down weeping, unable to understand why death is coming now. What can we answer? We cannot simply utter platitudes when we are honest and realize that the question is ours as well as the questioner's. Every day parishioners, students, readers ask me questions every bit as serious and I have become incapable of giving the textbook answers, the well-prepared reply. "Why do the righteous suffer?" "Why me?" "Why her?" people ask. Even the Book of Job is not entirely clear. Centuries of scholars equivocated and placed their differing answers at the end of the text. I have found that I can answer only by telling a story of a crucifixion, death, and burial and a mind-boggling resurrection. To questions about faith I answer with the story of Martin Luther at Worms or Dietrich Bonhoeffer at Flossenburg. With Bonhoeffer, the representative of the theological tradition I was born into with whom I can most identify, I can only confess: "Death is the supreme festival on the road to freedom." "This is the end, for me the beginning of life." "When Christ calls a man, he bids him come and die." [16]

To be brief, like Bonhoeffer I can only get my own story together and tell the great stories by which man has always lived and through which mankind never dies.

SEDATION AND INSIGHT

There have been any number of books on death and the dying in recent years. The psychology of death, as Ernest Becker has observed in *The Denial of Death*, has come into its own. Hundreds of conferences of ministers, physicians, and psychologists have been held upon this topic, including a featured address by Dr. Elisabeth Kubler-Ross at the 1973 American Academy of Religion meeting in Chicago. I cannot and do not intend to add anything to what Dr. Kubler-Ross has said in *On Death and Dying*, or that Becker has analyzed in his book and in his moving personal interview in *Psychology Today*. I do want to suggest that helping a person to sum up his life, to complete his story for himself may be the ultimate defeat of death that man seeks. To me this suggests that heavy sedation of the dying, beyond what is needed to make any pain tolerable, is inappropriate. Sedation may well cheat a person of the ability to make sense out of his experiences up to the final paragraphs, and by so doing cheat the person of the most transcendent experience of life.

We want to avoid what the writer of Ecclesiastes saw as the final absurdity of life.

For of the wise man as of the fool there is no enduring remembrance, seeing that in the days to come all will have been long forgotten. How the wise man dies just like the fool! So I hated life, because what is done under the sun was grievous to me; for all is vanity and a striving after wind. (Eccl. 2:16–17)

The preacher saw that the answer to this foolishness was the unfolding of things according to their time. He saw that it was the plot and the development of an individual life, of the history of society, and of the movement of the universe that gives sense to what happens. "For everything there is a season and a time for every matter under heaven: A time to be born, and a time to die." (Eccl. 3:1–2)

This is not an overwhelming shout of joy and triumph, but it is an affirmation of meaningfulness. It is perhaps the one pragmatic answer we can give to Shakespeare's incisive portrait of life as a meaningless moment upon the stage. Perhaps it doesn't matter if anyone else appreciates our performance as long as we do. Our life experiences clearly indicate that as long as we measure the quality of our story or performance by the reception of others, we are pretty much guaranteed a disappointment.

Awareness of the approaching end of our story and the impression we calculate that our total story will have upon the world is strongly indicated by the experiences of men and women who became world famous during their lifetimes. This kind of experience has been recorded of Harry S. Truman, Winston Churchill, and the psychologist Abraham Maslow. The editors of *Psychology Today* report the following message from Maslow, by way of a taped cassette, dictated just before he died.

I had really spent myself. This was the best I could do, and here was not only a good time to die but I was even willing to die . . . It was what David M. Levy called the "completion of the act." It was like a good ending, a good close. I think actors and dramatists have that sense of the right moment for a good ending, with a phenomenological sense of good completion—that there was nothing more you could add . . . Partly this was entirely personal and internal and just a matter of feeling good about myself, feeling proud of myself, feeling pleased with myself, self-respecting, self-loving, self-admiring . . .

My attitude toward life changed. The word I used for it now is the post-mortem life. I could just as easily have died so that my living constitutes a kind of an extra, a bonus. It's all gravy. Therefore I might just as well live as if I had already died.

One very important aspect of the post-mortem life is that everything gets doubly precious, gets piercingly important. You get stabbed by things, by flowers and by babies and by beautiful things—just the very act of living, of walking and breathing and eating and having friends and chatting. Everything seems to look more beautiful rather than less, and one gets the much-intensified sense of miracles.

I guess you could say that post-mortem life permits a kind of spontaneity that's greater than anything else could make possible.

If you're reconciled with death or even if you are pretty well assured that you will have a good death, a dignified one, then every single moment of every single day is transformed because the pervasive undercurrent—the fear of death—is removed. . . . I am living an end-life where everything ought to be an end in itself, where I shouldn't waste any time preparing for the future, or occupying myself with means to later ends . . .

Sometimes I get the feeling of my writing being a communication to my great-great grandchildren who, of course, are not yet born. It's a kind of an expression of love for them, leaving them not money but in effect affectionate notes, bits of counsel, lessons I have learned that might help them . . .[17]

MAKING A DECENT END

According to the *Pocket Data Book USA 1971*, the numbers of deaths (for 1968, the last year of record) in America totaled 1,930,000.[18] That is a lot of funerals. I cannot feel that all of these lives were frustrated, yet my own experience as a pastor tells me that many are cut short not by shortness of years but by failure to complete the inner story. Our society is not a philosophical or

meditative one. Few of us go out like Socrates, and fewer
still like Jesus Christ.

I often meditate upon both Socrates' and Jesus' deaths,
and bring these events to my students' attention. Socrates
was disturbed by the mourning of his disciples, saying:

"What is this strange outcry?" he said. "I sent away the
women mainly in order that they might not misbehave in this
way, for I have been told that a man should die in peace. Be
quiet, then, and have patience." [19]

And Jesus, hanging in agony and exhaustion upon the
cross, had lost none of what Schleiermacher called his
"God-consciousness." He was obedient and faithful unto
death—addressing God even in his cry of dereliction: "My
God, my God, why hast thou forsaken me?" (Mark 15:34).
And finishing: "Father, into thy hands I commit my
spirit." (Luke 23:46)

Making a good end to one's story is the most satisfying
experience in life. The richest, most creative life is not
necessarily fully told or on the right course according to
that person's inner story, as can be seen in Goethe's
deathbed request for "more light." Considering ourselves
as persons with stories, with rich inward lives, as spirits, if
you will, puts death in a different perspective. Looking at
life in this way, we can see that there is little or nothing to
be gained by keeping the physical body alive after the
mental life has ended. From my viewpoint heroic medical
and mechanical procedures that maintain heartbeat after
the brain's activity has dropped are sheer cruelty to the
survivors—since they add nothing to the person whose
inner story has ended.

I recall going to the university hospital in another city

with a student in my own school who had suffered a sudden cerebral stroke. Sitting with the heartbroken family for hours, waiting for the results of tests, trying to ease their pain baffled me. Then one of the physicians told me that the EEG, the electro-encephalograph's recording line, symbolizing brain activity, was flat. "How long has it been flat?" "Almost from the moment the boy was admitted," he answered. "Why don't you shut off the other machines, then?" I asked. "That's not for me to decide," he answered.

At least I had the hours of that night to try to prepare the family. Once the doctors told them of the situation, they agreed to "unplug" the heart, kidney, and other machines.

Men are more than physical signs, to be sure, yet there is little reason to think that the inner life goes on when brain activity ceases. Why torture the expiring or ourselves?

Men and women often come to an insight about their lives and the story they are telling themselves and the world. The most famous of such public utterances of insight, in my mind, is Dr. Martin Luther King, Jr.'s declaration, "I have a dream. . . ." King's dream included the very clear concept that the story he was working out in America might entail his own violent death. King's tremendous grasp of the transcendent symbols of our common religious and cultural heritage placed the whole movement for civil rights in perspective—and by touching responsive chords in multitudes made the movement effective. His "dream" seems to conclude that personal fantasy is a clue to history. While King did not want to die, he steadfastly refused to change his story— like Luther, Bonhoeffer, and Jesus Christ. Playing out your own personal story is precisely how history is made. A similar insight was operating in the late career of Robert Kennedy, as was a similar history-making courage.

I see the above experiences and the thousands like them throughout our society as a powerful reason for telling severely ill people that they are likely to die soon. Knowing the truth (as experts see it) about their chances may enhance the possibility of people's completing their own stories—to their own satisfaction—before the end. A story broken off in mid-sentence, a film marred at the close are aggravating not comforting experiences. I think, with Socrates, that a man should die in peace.

Epilogue

Throughout this book we have stressed the story quality of individual and social human life. Our way of being in the world, as persons, is the expression of the inner story we spend our whole life telling ourselves. Faithful attention to the inward fantasy realm and conscious understanding of the story we are telling is reflected in outward behavior; behavior that becomes the data of history. History, as a whole, is the unifying story that the human race has been telling through its billions of personal stories through millennia of time.

Nowhere does the basic importance of the personal inner story as a clue to understanding man and history become more clear than in religion. Confess with our lips what we will, deny what we deny, our religious stance in the world is the outgrowth of our inner story, the real locus of our concern, fears, hopes, and faith. Recently, theologians have become sensitive to the story quality of religion and the inward, personal character of faith. Numerous clergymen have come to the insight that the only real answer to religious questions is the telling of a story. Like Jesus, who said nothing to the crowds except in parables, we are thrown back upon the rich, inner life of personal fantasy and story. Like Jesus, too, the contemporary religious person must speak the truth, without dissembling, speaking with the authority of personal experience and not as a scribe.

In this book we have investigated some common types of personal fantasies or life scenarios, knowing in advance that we would not identify them all. How could we? No one knows everything, or even very much about the inner workings of another person's mind. We must proceed in such cases on the basis of our own experience and universalize only by analogy. Any logician will tell you that analogy is the weakest form of reasoning, but in such inward matters it is the best tool we have. To administer tests and questionnaires which could be quantified would not really be more objective or scientific. We still would connect the various reports people make by analogy, and finally by an analogy to our own experience.

Nonetheless, there do seem to be a few widely occurring types of life scenarios. Perhaps we have learned to see the "Wounded Healer" or the "Soldier of Fortune" in ourselves. Perhaps, too, we have gained insight into how our lifestyles are shaped by our inner fantasies. The philosophy of materialism is quite wrong; the mind and the spirit are not formed by the events in the material world, rather the material world is shaped by the inner world, which thinks, plans, and then does.

Fantasies also run in families. Not only do life scenarios fall into patterns; symbols and images, fairy tale plots and philosophical insights show similarities, too. The great religions of mankind emerge, under this form of analysis, as communities sharing similar stories, entertaining similar fantasies, and moved by similar symbols.

Literature, too, is the record of the inward human life. In poetry the message and medium are one and the same, the words or symbols tumbling out of the inner person, leaving a record for others of what one individual experienced behind doors of perception which no one else can enter. In novel and short story, drama and movie we can see the great thematic life scenarios developed and exposed for public wonder, inspiration, revulsion, and admonition. Aristotle was right in observing:

> Tragedy, then, is an imitation of an action that is serious, complete, and of a certain magnitude . . . in the form of dramatic action . . . through pity and fear effecting the proper purification of these emotions.
>
> And, . . . tragedy is an imitation, not of men, but of action and life, of happiness and misery. And life consists of action, and its end is a mode of activity, not a quality. Now *character determines men's qualities, but it is their action that makes them happy or wretched.*[1] (Italics mine.)

Great tragedy and literature in general therefore push our thoughts to the final truth about our inner stories, that the inward must be translated into the outward, that life must be lived out and our story fully told before it is ended by death. Our inward stories, confused and ill-developed, rise up demanding nourishment and completion, just as our physical bodies rebel against poor treatment by falling into disease. We fear death because we sense the insecurity of incompleteness. With Aristotle, we must recognize that death is not an evil but a chance to pull everything together, to finally realize all potentialities and possibilities in an ecstatic moment of fulfillment, for fulfillment is happiness. I hope this analysis has helped us all to recognize the unfinished task of storytelling that lies in the midst of most of our personal experience.

Albert Einstein once said that God may play his little jokes with the universe but he does not gamble. There is sense and even purpose in everything that is. The awesomeness of relativity does not deliver us into the darkness of chance, rather it relates everything to our thinking, observing, and acting selves. Religious leaders of all ages and groups have spoken of the plan of God. A plan is but a story one tells himself. Long ago, Bishop Berkeley declared that all of us are perceptions, thoughtful recognitions, if you will, in the mind of God. We are held in existence solely by the inward storytelling activity of Almighty God. Perhaps we are. Perhaps the Kingdom of God, the heavenly city of the philosophers, the classless society of the social critics, the marriage supper of the Lamb are all garbled versions of the story God is telling Himself. We can never be sure, certainly. We live by faith, seeing images and symbols, forms of men like trees walking, shadows flickering upon a cave wall, dimly apprehending the flow of history's story while we work out our own personal stories. Under such conditions of ignorance, risk, suffering, learning, adventure, and ecstasy, something in each of us responds to that which is by telling who we are. In the development of plot and the building of character, I hope we can say with the aged Paul: "The aim of our charge is love that issues from a pure heart and a good conscience and sincere faith." (I Tim. 1:5)

Notes

I. LIFE SCENARIOS

1. Hannah Arendt, *Between Past and Future: Eight Exercises in Political Thought* (Viking Press, N.Y., 1968).
2. Hans Ruesh, *Back to the Top of the World* (Charles Scribner's Sons, N.Y., 1973), p. 198.
3. Richard L. Rubenstein, *After Auschwitz* (Bobbs-Merrill Co., Indianapolis, 1966).
4. Harvey Cox, *The Seduction of the Spirit* (Simon & Schuster, N.Y., 1973); and *The Feast of Fools* (Harvard Univ. Press, Cambridge, Mass., 1969).
5. Mircea Eliade, *Patterns in Comparative Religion* (Meridian Books, World Publishing Co., N.Y., 1966); also see J. Kitagawa and C. H. Long, *Myths and Symbols: Studies in Honor of Mircea Eliade* (The Univ. of Chicago Press, Chicago, 1969).
6. Plato, *Phaedrus* (Bobbs-Merrill Co., The Library of Liberal Arts, N.Y., 1956), p. 265.

7. *Ibid.*, p. 244.
8. I have discussed the process of maturity accomplished through the acceptance of pain and defeat in *Religion After Forty* (Pilgrim Press, Philadelphia, 1973).
9. Hal Lindsey, *The Late, Great Planet Earth* (Zondervan Publishing House, Grand Rapids, Mich., 1970); also *Satan Is Alive and Well on Planet Earth* (with C. C. Carlson, Zondervan Publishing House, Grand Rapids, Mich., 1973).
10. Carlos Castañeda, *The Teachings of Don Juan: A Yaqui Way of Knowledge* (Ballantine Books, N.Y., 1968); and *A Separate Reality, Further Conversations with Don Juan* (Pocket Books, N.Y., 1972).
11. Arthur Miller, *Death of a Salesman* in *The Collected Plays of Arthur Miller* (The Viking Press, N.Y., 1957).
12. John Charles Cooper, *Finding a Simpler Life* (The Pilgrim Press, Philadelphia, 1974).
13. Information taken from a student survey made at Bowling Green State University, Bowling Green, Ohio, January, 1974.

2. CHANGING YOUR SCENARIO

1. Sam Keen and Anne Valley Fox, *Telling Your Story—A Guide to Who You Are and Who You Can Be* (Doubleday & Company, Garden City, N.Y., 1973). Copyright © 1973 by Sam Keen and Anne Bartlett. Used by permission of Doubleday & Company, Inc.
2. Annie Dillard, *Pilgrim at Tinker Creek* (Harper's Magazine Press, N.Y., 1974).
3. William Brandon, *The Last Americans* (McGraw-Hill Book Co., N.Y., 1974).
4. See Plato's Myth of the Cave in *The Republic*, Book VII, in *Plato*, trans. by B. Jowett, (W. J. Black, Inc., Roslyn, N.Y., 1942), pp. 398–428.
5. Alvin Toffler, *Future Shock* (Random House, N.Y., 1970).
6. Karl Menninger, *Whatever Became of Sin?* (Hawthorne Books, Inc., N.Y., 1973).
7. Carl Gustav Jung, *Memories, Dreams, Reflections*, recorded and edited by Aniela Jaffe (Vintage Books, N.Y., 1963), p. 133.
8. *Ibid.*, p. 161.
9. *Ibid.*, pp. 161–162.

10. *Ibid.,* p. 272.
11. *Nelson's Complete Concordance of the Revised Standard Version Bible,* compiled by John W. Ellison (Thomas Nelson & Sons, N.Y., 1957).
12. For Tillich's dream of his own death, see Rollo May, *Paulus, A Personal Portrait of Paul Tillich* (Harper & Row, N.Y., 1973), p. 104.

3. FAMILIES OF FANTASIES AND RELIGIOUS PHILOSOPHIES

1. Arnold J. Toynbee, *A Study of History,* 12 vols. (Oxford Univ. Press, 1935–61).
2. See Paul C. Empie and William W. Baum, *Lutherans and Catholics in Dialogue: One Baptism for the Remission of Sins* (Publication Office, National Catholic Welfare Conference, 1312 Massachusetts Avenue, N.W., Washington, D.C. 20005).
3. Harvey Cox, *On Not Leaving It to the Snake* (The Macmillan Company, New York, 1967).
4. Paul Tillich, *The Future of Religions* (Harper & Row, N.Y., 1966).
5. Ralph Waldo Emerson, "Brahma," in *A Little Treasury of British Poetry,* edited by Oscar Williams (Charles Scribners' Sons, N.Y., 1951).
6. Jim Oaks Bryan, *Jesus was a Beatnik* (J.O.B. Publishing Company, Largo, Fla., 1960).
7. Albert Schweitzer, *The Quest for the Historical Jesus* (The Macmillan Company, N.Y., 1968).
8. Milton Rokeach, *The Three Christs of Ypsilanti* (Alfred A. Knopf, N.Y., 1964).
9. Carlos E. Castañeda, *Journey to Ixtlan* (Simon & Schuster, N.Y., 1973).
10. Eric Sloane, *An Age of Barns* (Ballantine Books, N.Y., 1974).
11. Fyodor Dostoyevsky, *Crime and Punishment,* trans. by Constance Garnett (Modern Library, N.Y., n.d.).
12. William Faulkner, *The Unvanquished* (Random House, N.Y., 1965).
13. John Charles Cooper, *The New Mentality* (Westminster Press, Philadelphia, 1969).

14. Herman Hesse, *Magister Ludi: The Glass Bead Game* (Holt, Rinehart & Winston, N.Y., 1970).
15. André Malraux, *Man's Fate* (Random House, N.Y., 1968).

4. TELL ME A STORY

1. Holden Village, a retreat center owned and operated by representatives of the three Lutheran denominational groups, is located at the edge of the Glacier Peak Wilderness near Lake Chelan, Washington.
2. Viktor Frankl, *From Death Camp to Existentialism* (*Introduction to Logotherapy*) (Beacon Press, Boston, 1963).
3. Peter Farb, *Word Play, What Happens When People Talk* (Alfred A. Knopf, N.Y., 1974), p. 222.
4. Philip Slater, *Earthwalk* (Anchor Press, N.Y., 1974), p. 11. To see the disasters brought on by insane fantasies, read *It Gave Everybody Something to Do* by Louise Thoreson with M. Nathanson (M. Evans & Co., Inc., N.Y., 1974).
5. *Ibid.*
6. *Ibid.*
7. Jan Morris, *Conundrum* (Harcourt, Brace, Jovanovich, N.Y., 1974), pp. 114–15.
8. Donald Bogle, *Toms, Coons, Mulattoes, Mammies and Blacks* (Viking Press, N.Y., 1973), p. 181.
9. Henry David Thoreau, *The Writings of Henry David Thoreau*, Vol. II (*Walden*) (Houghton Mifflin & Co., Boston, 1893), p. 100.
10. See John C. Cooper, *Finding a Simpler Life* (Pilgrim Press, Philadelphia, 1974).
11. Don Biggs, *Breaking Out . . . Of a Job You Don't Like . . . And the Regimented Life* (David Mackay Co., N.Y., 1973), p. 2.
12. Slater, pp. 194–99 and *passim.*
13. *Ibid.*, p. 197.
14. Marge Piercy, *Small Changes*, inside front dust jacket.
15. *Ibid.*, pp. 28–29.
16. Rosemary Haughton, *Tales from Eternity* (Seabury Press, N.Y., 1973), pp. 84–85 and *passim.*
17. *Ibid.*, p. 87.

18. J. Martin Bailey and Douglas Gilbert, *The Steps of Bonhoeffer, A Pictorial Album* (The Macmillan Co., N.Y., 1969).
19. *Ibid.,* p. 39.
20. The Popular Culture Association, Bowling Green State University, Bowling Green, Ohio.
21. Harold Mendelson, *Mass Entertainment* (College and University Press Services, Inc., New Haven, 1966), p. 68.
22. Stephen C. Holder, "The Family Magazine and the American People," *The Journal of Popular Culture,* Fall, 1973 (VII:2), p. 264.
23. Keen & Fox, pp. 97–98, and *passim.* Also see John K. Bontrager, *Free the Child in You* (Pilgrim Press, Philadelphia, 1974).
24. Marcus Aurelius, *The Meditations,* No. 23 (Classics Club Edition, Walter J. Black, Inc., Rosylyn, N.Y., 1945).
25. Richard Adams, *Watership Down* (The Macmillan Co., N.Y., 1974).
26. Robert F. Capon, *Hunting the Divine Fox* (Seabury Press, N.Y., 1974), p. 5.

5. MAKING A GOOD END

1. "Death Doth Defer," by Peter Koenig, *Psychology Today,* November, 1972, p. 83.
2. Plato, *The Apology,* in *Five Great Dialogues* (Walter J. Black, Inc., Roslyn, N.Y., 1942), pp. 58–59.
3. *Ibid.,* p. 47.
4. Plato, *The Phaedo,* in *Five Great Dialogues,* pp. 152–53.
5. William Shakespeare, *Macbeth* in *A Little Treasury of British Poetry,* p. 105.
6. *Ibid.*
7. John Keats, in *A Little Treasury of British Poetry,* p. 382.
8. T. S. Matthews, *Great Tom* (Harper & Row, N.Y., 1974), p. 95.
9. Stewart Alsop, *Stay of Execution* (J. B. Lippincott, Philadelphia, 1973), p. 11. Note: Alsop died on May 26, 1974.
10. Ernest Becker, interview by Sam Keen, "The Heroics of Everyday Life: A Theorist of Death Confronts His Own End," *Psychology Today,* April, 1974. Note: Becker died on March 6, 1974.
11. *Ibid.,* p. 72.
12. *Ibid.*
13. Matthews, *Great Tom,* p. XVII.

14. Mark Twain, *The Mysterious Stranger*, edited by William M. Gibson (University of California Press, 1970).
15. See John O'Hara, *Appointment in Samarra* (Modern Library, N.Y., 1953). The legend is from the play *Sheppy* by W. Somerset Maugham.
16. Bailey and Gilbert, *passim.*
17. Reprinted from *Psychology Today*, August 1970. Copyright © 1970 Ziff-Davis Publishing Company. All rights reserved.
18. *Pocket Data Book USA, 1971* (U.S. Government Printing Office, Washington, D.C., 1971).
19. Plato, *The Phaedo* in *Five Great Dialogues*, p. 152.

EPILOGUE

1. Aristotle, *Poetics* in *Aristotle: On Man in the Universe* (Walter J. Black, Inc., Roslyn, N.Y., pp. 424–425.